FIRST PEOPLE

Also by Andrew Smith

Pastoralism in Africa: Origins and Development Ecology
(1992)

The Khoikhoi at the Cape of Good Hope:
17th Century Drawings in the South African Library
(with RH Pheiffer)
(1993)

Einiqualand: Studies of the Orange River Frontier
(1995)

The Cape Herders: A History of the Khoikhoi of Southern Africa
(with E Boonzaier, P Berens and C Malherbe)
(1996)

The Bushmen of Southern Africa: A Foraging Society in Transition
(with C Malherbe, M Guenther and P Berens)
(2000)

African Herders: Emergence of Pastoral Traditions
(2005)

Excavations at Kasteelberg, and the
Origins of the Khoekhoen in the Western Cape, South Africa
(2006)

The Origins of Herding in Southern Africa:
Debating the 'Neolithic' Model
(2014)

FIRST PEOPLE

PEOPLE

The Lost History of the
KHOISAN

Andrew Smith

JONATHAN BALL PUBLISHERS
CAPE TOWN • JOHANNESBURG • LONDON

Published in South Africa in 2022 by
JONATHAN BALL PUBLISHERS
A division of Media24 (Pty) Ltd
PO Box 33977
Jeppestown
2043

Reprinted once in 2022 and 2023

ISBN 978-1-77619-159-8

ebook ISBN 978-1-77619-160-4

Every effort has been made to trace the copyright holders and
to obtain their permission for the use of copyright material.
The publishers apologise for any errors or omissions and would be
grateful to be notified of any corrections that should be incorporated
in future editions of this book.

www.jonathanball.co.za
www.twitter.com/JonathanBallPub
www.facebook.com/JonathanBallPublishers

Cover images: Bushman rock art showing a boys' puberty
ceremony, Cederberg region, Western Cape (after Yates et al. 1990:
Figure 29)

Cover by publicide
Illustrations by David Maclennan
Design and typesetting by Martine Barker
Printed and bound by CTP Printers, Cape Town
Set in Baskerville

To Belinda and Alessandra

CONTENTS

FOREWORD

Not many South Africans understand the sheer scale of this country's human development and past, which stretches back to the early hominids of 3.5 million years ago. Archaeology is a complex discipline that through a detailed forensic process enhances our knowledge of past people, events and climates. Archaeological methods evolve over time as the discipline makes use of scientific discoveries to help it put together the jigsaw puzzle of the past.

This vast depth of South African archaeology is generally difficult for ordinary people to access, as the language in scientific journals and university-level textbooks is tiring to read, sometimes overly formal and uses terminology that is generally outside daily use. In some ways this has not only put people off but also given rise to half-truths and the development of alternative, untested histories, many of which are in circulation today.

In *First People: The Lost History of the Khoisan*, Andy Smith has wisely limited the time scale covered to the period in which we believe the ancestors of modern humans and the people of the Cape existed – a complex but fascinating period of our existence. In South Africa today there are actually a number of people and groups that are rediscovering a heritage that was effectively lost to the colonisation process. They are beginning to form groups as they rediscover their identity. A number of these groups are political in their agendas and are informed by hearsay and legend, while others are historically well-informed. At the bottom of this is the deep need for communities to re-discover history and identity – a very positive thing for society at large. The problem is that there are few up-to-date, modern history/archaeology books to assist communities to do this.

At last, we have a considerately written book that fills this gap in a major way. Not only does it abandon old colonial ideals and versions of the past, but it is also sensitively written and full of up-to-date knowledge on scientifically based find-ings and modern techniques. However, most important is the fact that *First People* is easy to read and accomplishes the almost impossible task of marrying academically based knowledge into a well-written and carefully executed book. It can be kept at home and read from cover to cover, yet would also be comfortable as a teaching book in a university or school. This book needs to find its way into family homes, school libraries and academic settings.

In a way, *First People* also parallels Andy Smith's life. He is an expert in the subject as a result of a lifetime of research, physical excavation and accumulation of knowledge, yet the book does not indulge in self-praise but gives knowledge to us all.

Tim Hart (MA)
Director of ACO Associates CC
Archaeology and Heritage Specialists

INTRODUCTION

The name 'Khoisan' was created to encompass the 'click-speaking' people of southern Africa assuming that they were all genetically connected, before it was recognised that there are three separate languages (two Bushman languages, and Khoe), all of them mutually unintelligible. These were the aboriginal hunters and herders of the subcontinent. The genetics of the San (or Bushmen) are the most complex and diverse in the world today. This means it is possible that they are ancestral to all living humans. The Khoekhoen were the herding people who introduced domestic animals and occupied the winter rainfall areas in the west that precluded the expansion of Bantu-speaking Iron Age farmers whose crops were summer rainfall. This book is dedicated to the descendants of these fascinating people who survive today, even though, in the 21st century, they are still pushed aside by black (beginning 5th century) and white (beginning 17th century) colonial interests.

My first experience with traditional herders was on the Persian Gulf coast in Iran in 1964 where I used camels and donkeys to get my camping gear and equipment to the top of the mountains to give offshore seismic operators a navigation fix during oil exploration.

In 1968, after I had finished my undergraduate studies at the University of California, Berkeley, I hitch-hiked from Glasgow, Scotland, where my parents were living, to Nairobi, Kenya, to meet up with one of my professors, Glynn Isaac. During my stay in East Africa I had the opportunity to visit Maasai homesteads (*manyattas*), my first contact with Africa's pastoral people. While in Nairobi, I got a message from one of my other professors, J Desmond Clark, inviting me to be part of the scientific contingent to the Ennedi Mountains of Libya to start at the end of the year (1969).

Unfortunately, Muammar Gaddafi seized power in Libya in September of that year and our plans had to change, so the expedition became the British Aïr Mountains Expedition to Niger. On this expedition I had my first contact with Tuareg herders, who helped us with finding camels and with the logistics of working in the Central Sahara. The excavations I conducted in Niger included work on early pastoral sites of the Sahara, and this became the focus of my doctoral research.

I was able to formulate an additional programme to do the second half of my thesis research, which I did in the Tilemsi Valley, north of Gao in Mali, in 1971. Again, I worked closely with Tuareg herders, and was able to learn a great deal about nomadic pastoralism.

On my return to Berkeley in 1971, I was invited by Desmond Clark to join an expedition to the Nile Valley, south of Khartoum, which took place in 1972.

I went to Ghana to teach at the University in 1973, and finished my Berkeley PhD thesis there, which was awarded in 1974.

I joined the Department of Archaeology, University of

Cape Town, in 1977. It was a natural step in South Africa to continue my research into herding societies there, and so began my interest in the Khoekhoen. I excavated at the richest prehistoric herding site in the Western Cape, Kasteelberg, on the Vredenburg Peninsula, between 1982 and 1992, and published a monograph on the work in 2006.

In 1993, I attended a month-long course on the Bedouin at Sde Boker in the Negev, Israel, meeting a number of the last transhumant herders in the country.

I worked with Richard Lee (University of Toronto) and Ju/'hoansi associates in northern Namibia in 1995 and 1997, doing archaeological excavation, while Richard gathered information on the Bushman history of Nyae Nyae from local elders.

In 2000, I was invited to be an expert witness at a court case in Cape Town on behalf of the Richtersveld community who were trying to claim aboriginal rights to their land from Alexkor Mine. The case was decided in favour of the community by the Constitutional Court in 2001.

In 2001, I excavated at Bloeddrift 23, a pastoralist site on the Lower Orange River in the Richtersveld, and that year I was also invited by Rudolph Kuper to join an expedition organised by the Arid Climate Adaptation and Cultural Innovation in Africa group from Cologne, Germany, to the Western Desert of Egypt, where we worked on prehistoric sites.

I subsequently surveyed archaeological sites in the Western Cape, and excavated the St Helena Bay skeleton, published in 2014 as 'First ancient mitochondrial human genome from a pre-pastoralist southern African'.

CHAPTER 1

Khoisan Peoples

[H]e saw the fate of history in popular culture as con-
ditional on its self-appointed masters being prepared to
reacquaint themselves with the imaginative skills of the
storyteller.

— *Simon Schama, in* The New Yorker, *1998*

'I've found one!' exclaims a young learner from a school in
rural South Africa on a field trip to see where Palaeolithic
stone tools come from. The learners have been given clues on
how to recognise flaked stone, and the site they are walking
across is an open path inside a nature reserve. Such excitement
underlines the fact that archaeology is everywhere, if you
know how to see it.

To this group of pre-teen children, these tools are a first
awareness of people in the distant past having lived in the
same space that they themselves inhabit today. The next step
is to ask how prehistoric people lived, and what would have
been important to them. To answer this question, one child
quickly says, 'Water' — and, yes, their stone tools are not far
from a permanent stream. Discussion about food, hunting and

1

gathering, then, is a logical addition to understanding the cultural ecology of early Khoisan people in their area, even if a time depth of 50 000 to 100 000 years might be difficult for them to envisage. Middle Stone Age artefacts dated to this period are widespread across the South African landscape, sometimes in the most unusual places, such as in the high country and on steep slopes.

The importance of leaving the stone tools where they are found is stressed by the archaeologist. The learners quickly understand that the tools are important clues to the past, and if removed without proper documentation and recording, would be lost to scientists in the future.

In this book I would like to introduce the archaeology and genetic background of the First People of southern Africa: the Khoisan. This is not purely an isolated academic exercise, as there is a good chance that we all, in our distant past, are ultimately descended from these people who lived at the southernmost end of Africa.

The Khoisan peoples of southern Africa have a long history of being pushed to the social periphery. The Bushmen were often considered as just animals who stole cattle, and so deserved to be shot, while Khoekhoen were regarded as convenient labour as herdsmen. In the 'new' South Africa Khoisan peoples have been pushed aside by 'black' aspirations, and no Khoisan language has been given the status of an 'official' language (even though the South African coat of arms bears a saying in a Khoisan language). There is a common complaint among Khoisan descendants: 'We were not white enough under apartheid, and are not black enough for the new South Africa'. So it is understandable that so-called coloured descendants of the Khoisan should feel marginal-ised. This is a theme that permeates all ex-colonial countries. The Aborigines of Australia, the Native Americans of North America and the isolated peoples of the Amazon also feel the heavy hand of historical colonial exploitation and neglect.

It is not always easy to bridge the gap between science and what the general public know about their society and where it comes from. There is a tendency for academics to focus too much on their closed world, as historian Yuval Harari describes: 'Scientists hope to dispel wrong views by better science education ... by presenting the public with accurate facts and expert reports ... Most of our views are shaped by communal groupthink rather than individual rationality, and we hold on to these views out of group loyalty ... Even scientists are not immune to the power of groupthink ... The scientific community believes in the efficacy of facts, hence those loyal to the community continue to believe that they can win public debates by throwing the right facts around, despite much empirical evidence to the contrary' (Harari 2018: 219–220).

There has been some attempt by archaeologists in South Africa to close the gap. John Parkington of the archaeology department at the University of Cape Town (UCT) and his colleagues at the Krakadouw Trust have made fine steps to open that part of the academy to a wider audience (Park-ington et al. 2015). It is over 90 years since Isaac Schapera (1930) wrote his seminal work on the social anthropology of the Khoisan. In the quarter century since the publication of *The Cape Herders* (Boonzaier et al. 1996), and later the compan-ion work on the Bushmen (Smith et al. 2000), ideas on Khoe-khoe history have changed. I am aware that we do not have all

3

the answers, and I hope that this book, designed for students and Khoisan descendants interested in early southern African history, will show how the research into their history keeps evolving in the 21st century. I will try to build up a picture of the archaeological, linguistic and genomic history to make sense of this complexity, and to describe the lives of these people, many of whom have lost their language and culture in the modern world. We are all the poorer for the loss of stories, experiences and skills that can never be replaced.

To develop this picture of the history of Khoisan people, we will travel back to the beginnings of early modern humans, then take a timeline to the direct Stone Age ancestors of the Bushmen and continue up to the present. We will look at the way of life of hunter-gatherers in the recent history of southern Africa, and then introduce the first herders who later became known as the Khoekhoen at the Cape. We also want to see what modern genomics can tell us about how the various linguistic and economic groups related to each other. Finally, we will ask about the Khoisan today, and where they find themselves in the modern world of independent African states.

Names

The names Europeans called indigenous people they met on their travels often were the result of assumptions created by ancient geographers, such as the Greek Herodotus (5th century BC) and the Roman Pliny the Elder (1st century AD), who attempted to describe the peoples who lived beyond the circum-Mediterranean (or the then known world). Such fantastic creatures were the source of myth, and many of those described were assumed to be Anthropophages (man-eaters). So influential were these early writers that their ideas held sway until the Portuguese voyages of exploration at the end of the 15th century.

In southern Africa, these assumptions also held, and the 'savages' described by the early travellers fitted their assumptions. Franck van der Does, who sailed on the *Hollandia* as part of the Cornelis de Houtman expedition of 1595, offered this description: '[W]e feared that ... the African savages would kill and eat us' (Raven-Hart 1967: 19).

The naming of southern Africa's First People was done by early colonists, and, of course, because it was written down, achieved authenticity (see Brink 2004). The names the various groups used for themselves would have been their own ethnonyms (who they were in their own language, usually at the band or group level). They seldom had general collective names, and these, when they existed, such as 'Khoekhoen = Hottentot', were usually seen as a shorthand by colonial interests. For example, Khoe means 'people'; therefore Khoekhoe means 'people/people', but with the subtext of 'real people', which they probably used to distinguish themselves from hunter-gatherers. Let us look more closely at these names.

Khoisan: What does this name represent, and where does it come from? The word was first coined in 1928 by Schultze as a way of collectively describing the click-language users of southern Africa. The assumption was that these people were in some ways connected to each other through their languages. This name was also used to mean the small, brown-skinned people who were quite distinct from black Africans, the

Bantu-speakers of southern Africa. Thus, it had both a genetic and a linguistic assumption built in. The word 'Khoisan' is a colonial artefact but is in common use by descendants today.

Recent research among linguists (Güldemann 2008) has shown that there are two distinct Bushman languages, Kx'a (Ju) and Tuu, which are mutually unintelligible, that is, they cannot speak to each other, and are genetically distinct. Khoe is a quite separate language group and may well have origins outside southern Africa.

Strandloper: This means 'beach ranger' and refers to foraging people living along the coast and subsisting off marine resources. They apparently had no domestic animals, so may have been either Soaqua or impoverished Khoekhoen.

Hottentot: This was the name given to the herders of the Cape by the Dutch. The derivation of the name is not clear, but it may have been a commentary on the clicks in their language. All Khoe groups had their own ethnonyms, for example Goringhaicona (!Uri-//'ae, a group living around the Cape Peninsula), Cochoqua (whose territory included Saldanha Bay), Chainoqua and Hessequa (who lived beyond the Hottentots-Holland Mountains), etc. These were clan names recorded at the time of the first colonial observers in the 17th century. These names would probably have been flexible, as there was a great deal of fluidity in who was the leader, and how the groups changed over time (for more detail, see Fauvelle-Aymar 2008).

Khoekhoen is the collective name used by the Nama-speakers of Namibia today, but variants include Khoikhoi and Quena. Khoekhoe would be the language spoken, and like

Khoe could be used as an adjective (Smith 1998).

Soaqua or Sonqua: These were hunter-gatherers without domestic stock. The name came from the Khoekhoen, meaning 'people of the bush', but it probably had a subtext meaning 'people unlike ourselves with no cattle', and who spoke a different language. Again, each group would have had its own ethnonym, but few of these were recorded by the Dutch at the Cape. An exception was probably Swy Ei or Oesjswana, the Sneeuberg Bushmen encountered by Colonel Robert Jacob Gordon in 1777. Their name might have been recognised as they were very effective in keeping the Dutch colonists out of their area for many years. At the Cape they probably spoke a Tuu language, like the /Xam of Bushmanland (Bleek & Lloyd 1911). The name 'Bushmen' is a direct translation from Khoe, and was the word used by the early colonists for southern African hunter-gatherers. Because it was deemed derogatory, some researchers prefer to use the name 'San', but this was the name given by the Khoekhoen (San-qua = bush people) and was probably equally derogatory when used by them. For the hunter-gatherers, I prefer to use the term 'Bushman' instead of 'San', because, in my experience in working with them in the field, this is the collective name they would use themselves.

Differences between Bushmen and Khoekhoen

Perhaps the most significant difference between hunter-gatherers and herders is in their social systems. Using examples of modern hunters in southern Africa, Alan Barnard (2002; 2007) shows the anthropological differences between what he calls the 'Mesolithic' (hunter) and 'Neolithic' (food producer) modes of thought, rather than modes of production. The differences are great, and include concepts of accumulation and consumption of resources, leadership, kinship models and how land is perceived and used. His examples are of modern hunters who are in transition in the 21st century to fit into the dominant societies around them.

A basic premise offered by Barnard (2007: 15) is the following:

> In broad terms, the foraging mode of thought is resilient and resistant to contact with agro-pastoralists. Typical characteristics of hunter-gatherer society include a band level of social organisation, large territory for size of population, lack of social hierarchy, universal kinship (everyone being classified kind of 'kin', no non-kin), widespread sharing, a dualistic mentality (farmers think in 'threes'), symbolic relations between hunted animals and humans, and flexibility in all realms.

There are two types of hunter-gatherers: 'immediate return' and 'delayed return' (Woodburn 1988). Kalahari hunter-gatherers are immediate return, as they go out to forage for food every day and store very little for future use. They are known for their egalitarianism, with no one person being above another socially. In fact, levelling is the way that people are kept in their place. Anthropologist Richard Lee spent many months working among the Ju/'hoansi of Nyae Nyae when he was doing his doctoral research in the early 1960s. To thank the people for their help and patience, Lee brought in a large fat ox as a gift. He was initially shocked by the response he got from his Bushman friends. They basically told him he was very ungrateful for all the trouble they had gone to, and totally denigrated the animal offered as something of such poor quality that it was beneath them. What Lee finally realised was that they had accepted him into their group and he was not to think of himself as better than anyone else by providing such a splendid animal. In other words, he was being 'levelled' (Lee 1969). This shows that no one within Ju/'hoansi society is a leader. No one makes decisions for the group. This is only done by talking ... and talking ... and talking until a consensus is reached. A hunter must show humility even when he has been successful. Often, other camp members have to work hard to get out of him what has happened, and where the dead animal is. No boasting allowed!

To put this into perspective: egalitarianism and levelling practices are not unique to southern African hunters. They are common features of immediate-return hunter-gatherers everywhere. If any resources can be accumulated, then social hierarchies can exist, as seen in delayed-return hunters. Wiessner (1996: 187) says that social restrictions have to be in place to force egalitarianism because, 'as the many levelling mechanisms in forager societies imply, the tendency of individuals to seek status and influence is a current that runs through all societies'.

To elaborate on delayed-return hunter-gatherers: these would be people who have a resource that could be stored for future use. It could be fish that is dried or smoked and kept until the dry season, or even traded for other food, as done by the coastal people of the Pacific Northwest of the United

States and Canada who harvest the salmon runs every year. This allows them to have big celebrations called 'potlatches', with status accrued through the success of these (Suttles 1960). Other examples might be the hunter-fisher shellfish collectors on the shores of Lake Victoria in Kenya, or the hunter-fishers of the Botletle River in northern Botswana. It has even been suggested that the huge accumulations of black mussel shells on the Cape West Coast, known as 'mega-middens', were left by foraging people who dried the mussel meat for delayed use or exchange (Henshilwood et al. 1994).

By way of contrast, pastoralists own animals, and are responsible for their wellbeing. The herders need to make sure the animals have enough pasture and water, and to keep them away from potential predators (both human and animal), disease vectors and harmful plants. Ownership also incurs wealth, as some herders could have more animals than others. If a herder has a very big herd, he may have to have someone to help with the needs of the animals, and the person he hires cannot consider himself an owner, and so might have lower status. We also know from the historical record that the Khoekhoen often had Sonqua as herdsmen, or at least as guards (Waterhouse 1932).

Early contact

The Portuguese sailor Bartolomeu Dias was the first European to meet the Khoekhoe herders of the Cape when he made landfall at what is now Mossel Bay in 1488. He called the place Angra dos Vaqueiros, or 'Bay of Cowherds', because of the large cattle herds he saw there. The first contact between Europeans and the hunter-gatherers of southern Africa probably occurred in November 1497 when members of Vasco da Gama's crew met several local men, including one collecting honey, at St Helena Bay on the West Coast. There is no mention of domestic animals having been seen by Da Gama or his crew, so this individual was most likely a coastal foraging Soaqua (Axelson 1973: 22), from a people later called Strandlopers. Of course, there was no language communication possible, but through the use of signs the Portuguese sailors understood the man to tell them that his people lived near some hills 'two leagues' distant (Raven-Hart 1967: 3). Excavation of some small rock shelters in the hills along St Helena Bay indeed has shown that there were people living there for many years (Smith 2006).

The small ships of Bartolomeu Dias had been travelling for six months when they finally made landfall at Mossel Bay. What has survived of his journal records that the local natives ran away from him. Nine years later Vasco da Gama, in what is known of his journal, informs us that Dias's crew had been taking water when they were attacked by the herders, who threw stones at the visitors – no doubt because of their bad manners in not asking permission first, as would have been expected among the Khoekhoen (see Schapera 1930: 225). Dias responded by firing a crossbow and killing one (Raven-Hart 1967: 5).

The very first contact between Europeans and Khoisan did not bode well for how colonists and local people would deal with each other in the future. Lack of communication and understanding on both sides was to continue, and little

11

Figure 1.1: *Adam and Eve*, engraving by Albrecht Dürer, 1504 (public domain).

information came back to Europe that showed any sensitivity about who the local herders were, or how they lived. This lack of sensitivity is expressed in a description by one of the earliest travellers, Giovanni da Empoli, in 1503:

Figure 1.2: Khoekhoen parents with child, woodcut by
Hans Burgkmair, 1509 (public domain).

The men have no hair; their scalps are scabby and ugly;
they have rheumy eyes, and their bodies down to the waist
are covered with shaggy hides. They carry their private
parts in a hairy pouch like a sheath always upright.

13

The women wear similar cloaks of skin, and to this they
attach a hairy tail from the same animal, which they wear
before and behind to cover their shame. They have very
long breasts which look very deformed. The men carry
darts with tips of iron, which someone has discovered.
They have no religion, eat their meat raw, so far as we
could see, they speak in their throat with many signs and
hissings, and we never succeeded in understanding a
word they uttered ... to sum up, they are a bestial people.
(Noonan 1989: 140)

Although the visitors thought the Khoisan were bestial,
they initially also saw them as living in a Garden of Eden, un-
touched by many of the problems that European Christianity
believed were created when humanity fell from biblical grace.
The depiction of the Khoekhoen illustrating the 1506 journey of Balthasar Springer to the Indies shows great similarities
to Albrecht Dürer's *Adam and Eve* (Figures 1.1 and 1.2), no
doubt because the artist, Hans Burgkmair, was part of the same
artists' club as Dürer in the German city of Augsburg, and the
Fugger family, also of Augsburg, were the bankers underwriting
the voyage (Smith & Pasche 1997). It is remarkable that Burgkmair's woodcut depiction is the first image known to have been
made of the Khoekhoen but it lacks the 'savage' elements all too
evident in many of the later images of the 16th and 17th centuries (Smith 1993). This fact is elaborated by Leitch (2009: 135)
in her analysis of the place of Burgkmair in the development
of ethnography: 'Burgkmair pushed the boundaries of print-
making ... advanced naturalism ... developed formulas for proportion ... that better render the empirically observed world ...

Using familiar iconographic models, he relativized his subjects to the European viewer by bringing them into line with recognizable narratives and European traditions. He familiarized Africans ... by endowing them with recognizable proportions, taking them out of the conventional categories of the exotic.' By making them recognisably 'human' to his European audience, Burgkmair was demonstrating that cultural difference could be comparable with similar universal categories on which ethnography would later be built.

This idyllic view of the Khoekhoen was not to last. In 1510, the soldier and explorer Francisco de Almeida, on his return voyage from India, made a stop at Table Bay. The Portuguese sailors badly wanted fresh meat, so in order to entice the local herders into giving them cattle, they kidnapped some children. This was a big mistake. The Khoe immediately responded by attacking the crew and managed to kill De Almeida and many of his men before the survivors made it back to their boats. The consequence of this was that the Portuguese avoided Table Bay for the next century, making their African headquarters on the East Coast at Delagoa Bay (today Maputo).

Almost 150 years later, the first long-term contact between Khoekhoen and Europeans was with the Dutch crew of the *Haarlem*, which was wrecked at Bloubergstrand in 1647. The 'Remonstrantie' of 1649 was a report by members of that group to the Heeren XVII, the board of directors of the Dutch East India Company (VOC), in Amsterdam. The report gave a very positive view of their relations with the Khoekhoen and was probably one of the reasons behind the company's decision to set up a refreshment station at Table Bay to supply ships sailing to and from the East Indies.

The colony at the Cape

The Dutch station established at Table Bay in 1652, under Jan van Riebeeck, was initially seen purely as a place to refresh ships outbound to or returning from the Far East, where spices, in high demand in Europe, could be obtained. There was little incentive at that time to establish a permanent settlement in southern Africa, as the attraction was only seen in the meat that could be exchanged with the Khoekhoen. It did not take the Dutch long, however, to realise that the Cape could be agriculturally productive, and the Heeren XVII gave permission for a limited number of 'free burghers' to be allowed to farm, as long as their produce would go to the VOC. The first were given land around Rondebosch and Newlands in 1657, but farmers had expanded as far as Stellenbosch by 1680, and on to Paarl by 1687.

Figure 1.3: Khoekhoe man helping a European farmer, late-17th-century drawing, National Library of South Africa (Smith & Pheiffer 1993: Plate 8).

Thus, the pasture lands of the Khoe around Table Bay were quickly taken over by farmers. This extended to the Overberg, beyond the Hottentots-Holland Mountains, after 1700. Not only was the land usurped, but gradually the cattle of the Khoe were either stolen or exchanged for non-productive goods, such as metals or alcohol. A crisis occurred in 1713 when a smallpox epidemic tore through the Cape Khoekhoen. This was viewed as some form of witchcraft by the Khoe, many of whom fled upcountry away from the Cape. Those who survived became a labour source for the colony (Figure 1.3).

Two wars were fought between the Khoekhoen and the early Dutch settlers, in 1659 and 1673. The Khoekhoen were the losers in both cases, but the outcome might have been very different if the assumptions on the part of the Khoe had not been that the wealth of the Dutch lay in their cattle, instead of in the mercantile empire that supported the VOC. Stealing cattle was not going to make the Dutch go away.

In the early 1900s, this same focus on cattle would undermine the struggle of the Witbooi Nama and Herero in German South West Africa against the German colonial forces. The indigenous herders were too absorbed in fighting among themselves over cattle raiding and pasture expansion to be aware of the greater threat from German imperialism (Gugelberger 1984). Had they presented a united front against the intrusion, they might have pushed the Germans aside, and avoided the Herero War of 1904 that resulted in the setting up of the concentration camps, which killed many Hereros.

It is important to note that virtually all the information on the Khoisan hunter-gatherers and herders of the Cape is one-sided. As the aboriginal people of southern Africa had no written language, all reports come from European observers – until much later, when local people learnt to read and write

Dutch. Although there were a few Khoekhoen who learnt to speak Dutch or English and acted as translators – for example, Autshumao, leader of the Goringhaicona, became Van Riebeeck's interpreter – literacy, however, only developed once mission stations were set up at the end of the 18th century, by which time many of the Khoisan groups had either disappeared or been absorbed into colonial society, speaking Dutch and adhering to Christianity. Very few Dutch colonists learnt to speak a Khoisan language because they found the clicks in the speech too difficult to master.

Mission stations

Because the emerging farmers in the colony regarded the Khoisan as basically subhuman in comparison with Europeans, there began the general treatment of them as virtual slaves, even though this was formally forbidden by the VOC. The loss of land, livelihood and language took such a toll on the Khoe that mission stations were set up, such as those founded by the Moravian Church or the London Missionary Society. The intention was primarily to convert the Khoisan to Christianity, but the missions set up in the 18th and 19th centuries were in fact havens for dislocated Khoisan forced to work for colonial famers (Figure 1.3). Along the South Coast these were mostly Khoekhoen.

One such haven was Genadendal, in the Overberg, which was first visited by the Moravian missionary Georg Schmidt in 1737. When he left seven years later, a few of his converts had become practising Christians. When the next group of

18

missionaries arrived, in 1793, there was just one Schmidt follower, a certain Lena, still able to read her Bible. In time Genadendal, under Moravian tutelage, became a major centre of learning and artisanship. It became the largest town of its kind after Cape Town, renowned for the skills it imparted, especially literacy, although a Khoekhoe language (probably local Chainoqua) was still spoken at the station until the middle of the 19th century. So adept were the Khoe at learning to read Dutch that it provoked the jealousy of the local colonial farmers, many of whom were illiterate.

The base of the Moravian Church was in the town of Herrnhut (today close to the border between Germany and the Czech Republic). At Genadendal, Khoe blacksmithing skills were so good that they made a very special and highly prized knife, which was called a 'Herrnhuter'.

Genadendal was often a stopping place for travellers going east. One such traveller was Lady Anne Barnard, the wife of the British colonial secretary, who stayed over in May 1798. In a letter home to England she wrote how wonderful the voices of the Khoekhoen were in the church. She also noted that the missionaries she met 'professed themselves perfectly happy in their situation, though it was by no means free from danger, not from the Hottentots, who loved them, but from the boors [*sic*], who were angry at their having come amongst them to teach the others how to be industrious and independent ... They (the farmers) did not care whether they (the Khoe) were enlightened or not, provided they were kept poor, lazy and subordinate ... the farmers had found the Hottentots more patient, tractable and laborious than the slaves of other countries they had bought – they also came infinitely cheaper to them'

Figure 1.4: 'Fytje, Bushman Girl at Bot River, 15 October 1850', sketch by Charles Davidson Bell (Bell Trust Collection, UCT).

(Lewin-Robinson 1973: 122). In 1815, when the clergyman Christian Latrobe visited Genadendal, the village had grown considerably since Lady Anne's visit, to 256 cottages. There were 300 children at a meeting, and 130 girls attended the school. Two local children were drawn by the artist Charles Davidson Bell during a trip to the Overberg in 1850 (Figures 1.4 and 1.5).

Figure 1.5: 'Boy at Genadendal, 17 October 1850', sketch by Charles Davidson Bell (Bell Trust Collection, UCT).

Racial 'othering'

We must recognise that the 'Hottentots' have a very important place in world history. As the earliest African herders encountered by Europeans, and people who were widely described in travel literature from the 15th century onwards, they became stereotypical 'natives'. So startling were the differences from

21

what was considered 'normal' European culture that even the descriptions of the monstrous races thought to exist beyond the circum-Mediterranean area were not enough to prepare the European mind for the reality. In mid-18th-century England, Lord Chesterfield said of one of his contemporaries, Lord Lyttelton, 'The utmost I can do for him, is to consider him a respectable Hottentot.' This meaning of 'Hottentot' became fixed in the imperial mentality, so that in the third edition of the *Shorter Oxford Dictionary* (1970) we see the word defined as 'a person of inferior intellect or culture 1726'. As Hudson says: 'Europeans needed to neutralise the ideological threat represented by the Khoikhoi, a programme that culminated in the development of the modern science of "race" ... and its corresponding ideology of "racism"' (Hudson 2004: 308). This was the origin of the ideology of social Darwinism of the 19th century as the European powers assumed their superiority and divided Africa among themselves.

Such imperial ideas were built on the idea of *terra nullius* (empty land), initiated in the 11th century when Pope Urban II issued a bull (official statement) that allowed the Crusaders to take over Islamic lands in the Near East. This idea entered European legal thinking and was later used by imperial forces to justify the occupation of lands, especially in Australia and Africa, that were used by nomadic people, and so were deemed empty and not productive in European eyes.

Not only was the name 'Hottentot' seen as derogatory, but the shortened version, 'hotnot', became entrenched in the South African colonial mind as the most insulting epithet. Gabrielle Ritchie (1990: 5) puts it succinctly when, quoting Francis Meli, she says that 'an aim of colonialism and its

Figure 1.6: A group of Khoe women, late-17th-century drawing, National Library of South Africa (Smith & Pheiffer 1993: Plate 5).

strategies was to "inculcate among the oppressed a feeling of inferiority towards and rejection of their own heritage and potential". This element of colonialist practise applies to the situation in which the word "hotnot" is regarded as insulting.'

This book is intended as an exercise in attempting to understand who the Khoisan were, using the fragmentary evidence available from the biased colonial records and what archaeology has discovered. We must recognise that the Khoisan have not disappeared. Their genetic descendants are still living at the Cape and in Namibia and Botswana, although the Cape descendants mostly speak Afrikaans or English. We hope to be able to offer to these First People of the Cape as full a picture as is possible. New evidence is appearing of the genetics of the populations at the Cape that will add an even greater dimension about who the Khoisan were (see Petersen et al. 2013).

CHAPTER 2

Modern Humans in Southern Africa: The Middle Stone Age and Later Stone Age

There is general agreement among all specialists that our early ancestors evolved in Africa, and genetic evidence suggests both East and southern Africa as being the source of all modern humans (Pickrell et al. 2012; Chan et al. 2019), although early *Homo sapiens* remains from Morocco, dated to 300 000 years, may indicate a more northern link (Hublin et al. 2017). Modern humans left Africa around 80 000 years ago to inhabit all of the Old World. Why there was an exodus of humans out of Africa at this time is unknown, but Schlebusch et al. (2020) note that there was probably a population reduction at this time. There was a similar drop in numbers among southern African humans, leading to the hypothesis that this coincided with adverse climatic conditions throughout Africa, putting stress on numbers and possibly forcing northerly humans to try to find more amenable environments.

The initial expansion from Africa was up through the Levant to Eurasia and along the coast to India, and ultimately to Australia. Occupation of Australia, however, required some form of sea transport, as the seas of Sunda and Sahul between

Indonesia and Australia are very deep, and no land bridge existed. This gives us some idea of how competent these people were. The occupation of the New World only began some 15 000 years ago once people had travelled across Asia and were able to cross between Siberia and Alaska using the land bridge formed when the sea bottom was exposed. At this time the sea level was as much as 130 metres lower than it is today.

To define what is meant by 'modern humans', or *Homo sapiens*, we need to look at several criteria, chiefly the fossil record and archaeology (ancient DNA, or aDNA, is not yet available for this time period, but we can assume it will be extracted from ancient skeletons as new techniques are developed). These criteria, of course, need to be framed within time. Radiocarbon dating has a 50 000-year limit, so recent developments in dating methods beyond the limits of established radiocarbon dating techniques, such as optically stimulated luminescence and thermo-luminescence, have given us a hold on when these distant relatives of all of us lived.

Fossils: The fossil record of the bones of early modern humans from the geological period between 300 000 and 200 000 years ago, known as the later Pleistocene, is not rich, but examples have been found throughout Africa. As noted above, the oldest currently recognised are the Jebel Irhoud specimens from Morocco, dated to 300 000 years. Very old specimens also come from southern Africa, including Florisbad in the Free State (260 000 years) (Figure 2.1); we might also add the extinct hominin Rising Star, in Gauteng (235 000 years), although it is not seen as being in the line of modern humans.

One criterion that defines *Homo sapiens* is the development and expansion of the brain (Bruner et al. 2017), a phenomenon

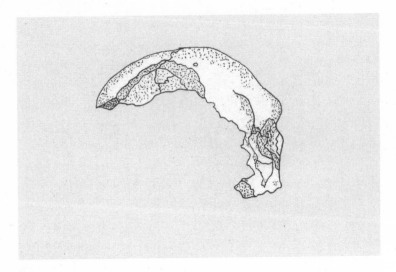

Figure 2.1: Skull cap from Florisbad: note the sloping forehead and heavy brow ridges (public domain).

known as encephalisation. This is most noticeable at the front of the skull where the frontal lobe that gives us our high foreheads (Figure 2.2) incorporated the huge brow ridges and sloping foreheads of our predecessors, seen in the Florisbad example (Figure 2.1). We also developed pointed chins that protrude below our mandibles (jaw bones).

Archaeology: Stone tools are by far the most common artefacts left by the first modern humans in Africa around 300 000 years ago. The tools that separate these mid- to late-Pleistocene people from earlier humans are called Mousterian in Europe, and Middle Stone Age in Africa. In these stone tools we see the beginnings of ballistic weapons in the form of spears. The spearheads were formed using a flaking technique known as 'Levallois', whereby the core from which they were removed

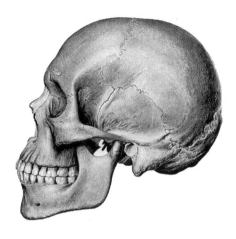

Figure 2.2: Modern human skull: note the high forehead and pointed chin.

was carefully prepared prior to the final point being struck off, or knapped. This means that the end product of the spearhead was already envisioned in the raw material by the tool maker before the final blow was struck. The cores show this careful preparation, and a skilful flake knapper could probably have removed several spear points from a single core before it was discarded and another chosen (Figure 2.3). The choice of raw material was also crucial in this exercise, and we see a preference for finer-grained rocks, such as quartzites and silcrete, at this time. Early bifacially flaked points are known as Still Bay, from sites on the Cape South Coast where they were first recognised.

It is during this long period that we see the first attempts at blade manufacture. This was a new technique whereby

Figure 2.3: Middle Stone Age disc core and flake from the Overberg: note the positive 'bulb of percussion' on the flake, and the negative on the core. This is the point at which the flake was struck and released from the core (Andrew Smith).

long slivers of stone were struck off a core that could be subsequently modified to create a wider and more specialised tool kit. Examples of this come from Canteen Kopje, in the Free State, and from Howiesons Poort, a cave near Grahamstown (today Makhanda) where the technique was first identified in the 1920s. Canteen Kopje is in the early part of the Middle Stone Age, and Howiesons Poort appears in the middle of the Middle Stone Age sequence, between 80 000 and 60 000 years ago, but it is replaced later by a cruder tool-flaking industry, although the blade manufacture still continues at a much lower frequency.

Although there are sites in the interior, some of the best-preserved sequences with fine artefacts are to be found all around the South African coast. This is a function of the sandstones of the coastal mountains, which form deep caves that were obviously attractive to early people. In these caves we also find the rhythm of sea-level changes during the Ice Ages, as the sea level rose and fell with the ice being trapped in the polar ice caps. This is reflected in how close the coast was at any moment in time. It is as part of these cycles that shellfish first show up in the caves, and it is also about this time that the human brain expands.

It has become widely known that omega-3 and omega-6 long-chain fatty acids are an important support for brain growth and function. These acids are to be found in shellfish and oily marine fish. The hypothesis is that the growth of the human brain may have been facilitated by intake of shellfish by women during pregnancy some 130000 years ago (Broadhurst et al. 2002). While the argument may seem facile, it is all too convenient that there is a conjunction with the time when shellfish first show up in the archaeological record of coastal caves. Klein and Steele (2013) show that the size of shellfish species was larger during the Middle Stone Age, getting smaller during the Later Stone Age. This they attribute to increasing population growth and heavier predation on shellfish during the latter period. Probably the brain was on a growth trajectory anyway, but perhaps it got a bit of a boost from shellfish eating?

We also have to consider when the shift took place from

male dominance in society, as seen in the larger non-human primates, such as gorillas and chimpanzees, to egalitarian societies, such as modern hunter-gatherers. Did it happen along with alloparenting, that is, the increased role of grandmothers in looking after young children while their daughters went plant collecting? Another point to consider is that increasing brain size and bipedalism (walking on two legs) in humans often meant difficulties in childbirth. Thus, it became necessary to have support from other women in the group – another socially binding mechanism (Rosenberg & Trevathan 1996). All of this would have had profound influence on how the human family developed.

It is possible that social organisation laid the basis of what we think of as 'human': mate selection to form stable nuclear groups, and gender roles in food acquisition, with men hunting and women gathering. If the shellfish scenario can be transferred back to this period in the Pleistocene, this would have been women's work, done while they looked after children, by contributing the consistent and dependable food base (plants constitute, on average, 60 to 70 per cent of the food brought back to base by Ju/'hoansi; Lee 1979: 450) but augmented by meat when men were successful in hunting. This food would have been brought back to a base camp for sharing, with all members, young and old, partaking. Survival required group effort.

The growth of the brain and human ability at this time produced some remarkable results in material preparation. In stone, people learnt to increase the flaking quality of the raw material by heating it in a fire (Schoville et al. 2017). They also used red ochre (iron oxide) to prepare a mastic or glue to firmly fix spear points onto shafts. Red ochre was also intentionally engraved at Blombos (Henshilwood et al. 2011) more than 70000 years ago. At this same site, on the southern coast near Still Bay, were found small sea shells with holes in them, suggesting that they were strung together, possibly as a necklace. At Diepkloof, on the West Coast near Elands Bay, a fine and almost complete cultural sequence from the Middle Stone Age has decorated ostrich eggshell showing up at around 60000 years ago. The first bone points appear around the same time, possibly being used as needles or as points for ballistic weapons.

Intentionality is seen as the earliest indication of 'art', or conscious decoration outside the body, a direction from which modern humans would increasingly demonstrate their aesthetics. Ochre could have been used initially as body paint, or to decorate other materials, such as skins. Through time, this would be found in the fine rock paintings of the Later Stone Age. Ochre has also been shown to be an effective sunscreen.

Middle Stone Age people were probably little different from us. They were intelligent, capable of hunting and bringing down animals much larger than themselves, in contrast to their predecessors who had to rely on big cats, from whose kills people could scavenge, or natural conditions, such as swampy ground, to immobilise meat sources any bigger than 50 kilograms. Due to the use of ballistic weapons, the hunting of eland and buffalo became common practice on the coastal plain, which was exposed by a drop in sea level of up to 130 metres before the Last Glacial Maximum (LGM), 18000 years ago.

The Later Stone Age

The transition from Middle Stone Age to Later Stone Age is an archaeological distinction primarily based on stone tool types recognised in the 1920s (Goodwin & Van Riet Lowe 1929). The technology of Levallois/prepared-core technique gave way to blade tools, whose precursors we have already seen in Howiesons Poort. These were smaller tools, embedded in wood hafts to make scrapers, saws and borers, as well as arrow tips for a developing ballistic weaponry.

These technological changes are signs of increasing sophistication in the use and exploitation of a wider set of resources, both in hunting and gathering. At the end of the Pleistocene, as the polar ice caps melted, changing sea levels altered coastlines, giving rise to different habitats. This is reflected in the existence of shell middens close to the present coastline, and in a fauna less dominated by large grazers, such as eland, which were previously found on the coastal plain formed by the low sea level, as well as in an increasing use of marine animals and birds, and less reliance on scavenging. These hunters would have been the direct physical and technological ancestors of the Bushmen.

The environmental conditions prevailing during the development of the Middle Stone Age to the early Later Stone Age mean that this was possibly a time of hardship in southern Africa for those living in the interior. Since very few archaeological sites dating from between 40 000 and 30 000 years ago have been found away from the coast, it may be an indication of lower numbers of people (Klein 1989). Alternatively, this was an Ice Age, so it was very cold. When sea levels dropped up to 130 metres, it is highly possible that humans migrated to the coast, which was as much as 100 kilometres further out than today. These sites, in consequence, are all under water today.

Another interesting observation is that early Later Stone Age people became much more skilful in exploiting their environment. Klein (1983) shows the changes in the kinds of large animals targeted from before the Ice Age started, around 80 000 years ago, to what happened after the ice had melted, allowing the sea to rise, some 12 000 years ago. During the pre-glacial period, eland dominated the large mammal bones found at Klasies River Mouth Cave along the South Coast (71 per cent), compared with only 26 per cent buffalo and 2.7 per cent bushpig. After the Ice Age the figures shifted, and at Nelson Bay Cave, also on the South Coast, eland represent only 7 per cent, but buffalo had increased to 47 per cent and bushpig to 46 per cent. This is interpreted as a trend towards more skilful hunting of dangerous animals, such as buffalo and bushpig, that are very difficult to get close to in order to make a strike with just a spear. In other words, this probably means that the bow and arrow (possibly with poison) had been invented. Although no bows have been found on archaeological sites, since these would have been made of materials that have disappeared, it was initially assumed that the tiny flaked pieces of stone that appeared around 20 000 years ago, quite different in size from the much larger Middle Stone Age spear points, would be indicators of arrowhead tips possibly used with poison. Careful study and measurement of bone points from a number of sites across South Africa by Lombard (2020a) indicates that some of these bone points, which had already been used during

the Middle Stone Age some 60 000 years ago, may well have
been poisoned, possibly as far back as 40 000 years. Similarly,
a follow-up study by Lombard (2020b) on Middle Stone Age
microlithic stone tools of the same age found traces of poison.
This was interpreted as evidence for the use of bows in this
period, although probably not as frequent as by hunters in the
Later Stone Age.

This may have been the case along the shifting coastline. In the interior were antelope, such as springbok, which
migrated in large herds. A different strategy would have been
used, possibly involving the use of stone-walled traps on the
migration route to focus the animals for the kill (Van der Walt
& Lombard 2018).

The height of the Ice Age, or Last Glacial Maximum
(LGM), some 18 000 years ago, may have caused serious population pressures and decreasing numbers of people. Certainly,
there are again few sites in the interior from 19 000 to 15 000
years ago. The numbers increase around 13 500 years ago
(Mitchell 2002), and this may correspond to what geneticists
have seen as the first population expansion of mitochondrial
(mtDNA) LOd1 around 14 000 years ago (Schlebusch 2010).

There is no question that the stone tool kit of Later Stone
Age hunter-gatherers was much more complex than what
had been found earlier in the Middle Stone Age. Blade production allowed the fabrication of small tools, which then
could be hafted for more efficient use. During the Middle
Stone Age one tool probably performed several functions,
such as cutting, scraping and boring. The Later Stone Age
tools became more specific to use, with fine-grained stone,
and because they were smaller the raw material began to be

Figure 2.4: Coastal foragers at the mouth of the Orange/ Gariep River in the 1780s (Gordon Archive, Rijksmuseum, Amsterdam).

moved over considerable distances. In addition, bone tools increased in variety, some even becoming barbed, probably for fishing. We only have glimpses of other organic materials being used, as these seldom survive for very long. Occasionally, pieces of plant material, such as wood or fibre, tell us about arrow shafts, or netting used for carrying goods, as seen in the picture Colonel Robert Gordon drew at the mouth of the Orange/Gariep River in the 1780s, showing a woman carrying ostrich eggs (Figure 2.4). Note also the whalebone structure of the hut, and the whale-vertebrae seats. Similar hut structures have been found further north on the Namibian coast (Smith & Kinahan 1984).

Rising sea levels after the LGM some 18 000 years ago

eventually meant that the oceans reached their present height. Over the last 9 000 years the coastline has remained roughly unchanged, and thus along virtually every rocky point one finds shell middens left over when coastal foragers discarded the empty shells. The middens can be in open areas or in deep caves, which can be dated. These are remarkable archaeological sites. The shells last for a very long time, and so offer us an excellent window into the activities of earlier people during the Later Stone Age. One interesting piece of information is the incidence of whale barnacles (*Coronula* spp). These shells only grow on the face of the Southern right whale. Since there is no evidence that these early hunters had boats, this means they did not hunt the whales, but had to rely on beached whales to get access to their meat. People eating whale meat would have had a hard time carrying the huge bones of these animals back to their campsites. The incidence of whale barnacles on archaeological sites indicates that chunks of whale meat, with the barnacles attached, were probably cut off to be consumed back in the domestic space. Without the barnacles being found on the sites, we could only guess about whale meat consumption.

The Later Stone Age set the stage for the modern hunter-gatherers of southern Africa. Their skill set was being fine-tuned to be able to harvest what the environment offered. All the available ecological niches would have been filled, particularly the rich coastal areas. But knowing how to live in the dry interior requires other skills, and since much of what we know of the modern hunter-gatherers comes from these regions, we can only surmise how closely humans had become integrated into the wider world they knew and seem to have respected.

CHAPTER 3

Hunter-Gatherers
in the Southern African Landscape

To get some sense of how hunter-gatherers perceive their world, we need to get away from the idea of environmental exploitation to control resources. The idea of 'sport' hunting does not make any sense to the Bushmen, although they will gladly eat any meat offered. In other words, there is a need to avoid the separation between humans and the natural world, and, perhaps even more importantly, the spiritual world. Prey animals are said to 'offer' themselves to the successful hunter. Some hunters say they can 'feel the movements of the animals sympathetically as beatings and tappings beneath their own skin' (Riley 2007: 298). Important rituals need to be performed to ensure that the animals share this idea.

The landscape in the mind of the hunter

To hunters, the landscape is an organic space of which they are an integral part – redolent with power, good and bad, that needs to be dealt with if the hunter is to be successful. Hunters know how to treat the landscape and the spirits properly, even under the harshest conditions, such as drought.

The landscape of the hunter is also criss-crossed by tracks, although less so than for pastoralists, whose cattle will follow worn paths that connect homesteads. The hunter's tracks may well be game paths, but they connect different places (or points) that are all known to the social group. In fact, they could be a shorthand in storytelling that connects the dots of the narrative. This is very different from a metaphorical view of how the landscape might be seen by non-hunters.

All this appears to exist in the stories and information given to Wilhelm Bleek and Lucy Lloyd by the /Xam Bushmen of the northern Cape in the late 19th century (Riley 2007). What seems to be a strong underlying factor is the high degree of negativity in the stories given by these hunters, indicative of the historical moment when they were under immense pressure from outsiders, who really only wanted to exploit the environment (through over-hunting of migratory game animals), rather than nurture and conserve it, as the /Xam would have done. This despoliation was highly indicative of the colonial mentality to 'rape' the land and its resources (including its people).

While most of the landscape 'points' might be difficult to recognise without a knowledgeable informant, some may be more obvious (such as rock art, water points, hunting hides, funnels for game trapping, etc.).

Would identifying the points and connecting the dots through a detailed survey using GPS or Google Maps allow some statement to be made about what the landscape may have meant in the mind of the hunter?

Landscape and memory

In *Landscape and Memory*, a monumental survey of the European relationship to landscape in culture and art, historian Simon Schama asserts:

> For if the entire history of landscape in the West is indeed just a mindless race toward a machine-driven universe, uncomplicated by myth, metaphor, and allegory, where measurement, not memory, is the absolute arbiter of value, where our ingenuity is our tragedy, then we are indeed trapped in the engine of our self-destruction. (Schama 1995: 14)

Schama goes on to argue against this in a long treatise in which he tries to demonstrate that Europeans have an almost primordial connection with landscape – forests, rivers, mountains – whose trajectory can be followed in art. He begins with the Romans and the Germanic tribes, the latter being seen as people of the forests. What Schama seems to have missed is that the Germanic tribes were farmers who used the forest as a refuge from the depredations of the Romans. Farmers are descendants of the earliest agents of environmental manipulation, and thus their landscape was often an artificial one. The Germanic tribes were therefore no different from the Romans, except they were not quite as efficient at changing their environment.

Landscape archaeology is an important way to place prehistoric people within their surroundings, being conscious that the landscape is more than just where people

39

lived and procured their food. People often leave important monuments that are clues to religious or symbolic meaning in the lives of past inhabitants. This can be easily seen with farmers who were closely attached to their land; being sedentary in most cases, they built up significant identity points reflecting the ownership of the land and its procreation, often with the help of ancestors whose graves may be sites for the performance of rituals.

But what about mobile hunter-gatherers and herders? Would places in their landscape show similar identifiable traces of belief? This appears to be a lacuna in the African ethnographic record, where research on hunters and herders has been detailed and extensive. What is missing is how these nomads perceived their place in the landscape, and where it might have meant structuring their world view.

Where this can be seen, however, is in the studies of Australian Aborigines, whose Dreamtime myths are invariably intertwined with landscape features identified with the activities of the ancestors. Ingold frames this way of perceiving the world by hunters:

> [S]ongs, stories and designs serve to conduct the attention of performers *into* the world, deeper and deeper, as one proceeds from outward appearances to an ever more intense poetic involvement. At its most intense, the boundaries between person and place, or between the self and the landscape, dissolve altogether. It is at this point that, as the people say, they become their ancestors, and discover the real meaning of things. (Ingold 2000: 56)

The people of Western Australia 'say that the landscape was formed, once and for all time, through the activities of theriomorphic beings, ancestral to humans as well as to all other living things, who roamed the earth's surface' (Ibid: 52).

In southern Africa, something similar is seen in the therianthropic figures (people with animal heads, such as elephant or antelope) on the rock walls of caves envisioned by trancers in their visits to the spirit world. Stories include landscape features, such as the /Xam story of the lizard that broke in two, which is identified with the Strontberg in Bushmanland (Deacon 1986). In addition, as Silberbauer (1981: 193) says: 'The boundaries of a territory are roughly defined by landmarks or, more correctly, in terms of areas surrounding these landmarks.'

Suzman notes the following about the hunter-gatherers of Nyae Nyae in Namibia:

> Foraging Ju/'hoansi don't animate their environment ...
> They also don't talk about animal spirits or speak of conscious, living landscapes ... they describe their environment's providence in more matter-of-fact terms: it is there and it provides them with food and other useful things, just as it does for other species ... it can sometimes be austere ... (but) ... they do not think of their environment as a 'thing' capable of agency ... Ju/'hoansi describe it as a set of relationships between lots of different things capable of agency – plants, insects, animals, people, spirits, gods and weather – that interact with one another continuously on what Ju/'hoansi called the 'earth's face'. (Suzman 2017: 106)

41

While Suzman's assessment may be true at the level of pragmatic food procurement, there is little separation of the 'spirit' and the 'real' world, and the hunters see the environment as full of stories. The environments of the Ju/'hoansi of Nyae Nyae and the /Xam of Bushmanland are redolent with tales of things that happened, which become guides to telling each other where to locate food, be it an animal that has been killed or plants that are ready for harvest. If a hunter kills an animal, he must not boast about it because this would be seen as trying to be better than everyone else. He must only let on, through innuendo and circuitous discussion, that it has happened. Once it has been established that the animal 'has died', then other men need to know where to find it so they can try to beat the carnivore competitors to the meat.

Nomads know the terrain in detail. The Inuit of the Arctic know conditions so well that younger men with their GPS units and snowmobiles, who could take the direct route between two points, might find that it was much slower than the route chosen by older men who know the snow, even though the distance is much greater (Aparta & Higgs 2005). Tuareg camel herders of the Sahel live in sandy plains dotted with small acacia trees that make distances difficult to judge. While the landscape may look featureless to the outsider, the Tuareg never get lost. The Ju/'hoansi hunters can communicate landscape information so precisely that there is no difficulty describing where an animal has been killed.

Figure 3.1: Nineteenth-century hunters in a cave: note
the spare arrow points in the headbands. Sketch by Charles
Davidson Bell (Bell Trust Collection, UCT).

Hunting technology

The Bushman bow and poison arrow is not a power weap-
on. This is why the bow looks rather frail, compared with the
traditional longbow of the English archers who were part of
Henry VIII's flagship, *Mary Rose*, which sank in the Solent
off the Isle of Wight in 1545. The skeletons of the archers
from the ship could be identified by the massive attachment of
sinew to their forearms, created by pulling these powerful
bows. The Bushmen did not need such power, as the force
of the arrow was not needed to kill. This depended on the
poison. The arrow was made in three parts: the reed shaft;

a link shaft (a piece of bone); and the point. The arrow was designed so that if it entered the skin of the prey animal, and the animal ran off into the bush, the shaft could be separated from the point as the prey moved through the bushes, leaving the poisoned arrow point stuck in the animal and allowing the poison time to work. The arrow shaft could then be reloaded – using the spare arrow points visible in the headbands of the hunters in Figure 3.1.

Hippo traps

Hunting hippos was not only hard work but also very dangerous. All the animals had to do was submerge themselves in the pools where they lived; if caught on land, they were ferocious fighters. To trap these huge animals, a very deep hole was dug along the track the hippo would use when foraging in the evening away from the river. These holes, probably at least five metres deep, had a stake planted upright in the middle. The hole was then disguised with saplings and brush. If a hippo fell into the hole it would be impaled on the stake. The animal would then be left until it died. Colonel Robert Gordon, head of the garrison at the Castle, Cape Town, found this to his peril when he fell into a hippo trap in the Eastern Cape on 24 December 1777 (Raper & Boucher 1988: 124). He managed to scramble out by standing on the back of his horse, but the horse died. Gordon thought that it had suffocated from the dust that blew up in the hole, but it probably was impaled on the stake. The amount of meat to be gained from trapping a hippo was well worth the effort to dig such deep holes.

Desert kites

In the early 1990s, while working in Bushmanland, south of the Orange River near Kakamas, I recognised stone walling that I suggested was a means used to channel herds of antelope towards hidden hunters who would then spear or shoot the animals with bows and arrows (Beaumont et al. 1995: Figure 6.5). Subsequent work (Van der Walt & Lombard 2018) has shown that similar structures exist north of the river, near Keimoes. These new finds have been equated with similar funnels known from the Near East, and referred to as 'desert kites', which they look like from the air where they were first seen.

These stone walls are substantial structures of boulders, which would have required significant effort to build. The southern structure is about 50 metres long, while some of those north of the river are over 100 metres. The inference is that it was worth the effort to build substantial stone walls, which probably meant that this location was on the migration routes of herd animals. The Y-shaped structures would have been a way of manipulating the landscape to facilitate hunting success by driving the animals into the arms of the trap. This was also made easier by the planting of feather bushes in the ground, and by having women and children wave similar plants in the air to focus the animals into the traps, where the men were hiding (Riley 2007). The traps were built on a slope just below the skyline, so that they were invisible to the prey animals until they were on them. The hunters could hide behind semicircular stone enclosures (Smith & Ripp 1978: Figure 5) or dig shallow holes in the ground where they would not be seen by the animals

(Riley 2007). Enormous herds of springbok regularly moved across these open plains, as described by Dunn (1873: 31): 'We have driven through them for six hours (35 miles), while from reliable information, they extend for one hundred miles in length. Imagine flocks of from 2 000 to 6 000 of these animals scattered over the plain at intervals of two to three miles apart.' Similar use of the terrain has been suggested at a site I was working on north of Vanrhynsdorp, where stone tools were found not on top of a dune but just below it. If the hunters had been on the skyline, they could be seen, but just below they were part of the dune.

Tracking skills

One day, sitting in his Land Rover at the edge of a waterhole, Dr Flip Stander observed some wild dogs trying to drag a dead buck out of the water onto a rocky rim. They had partially achieved this when a lion approached and chased the dogs away. The lion ate some of the buck. Stander then brought the Bushmen who worked for him to the waterhole and asked them to read the sign left by the animals. In spite of the rocky surface that surrounded the waterhole, there was enough sand covering to leave spoor in several places. The Bushmen were able to reconstruct the sequence of events with 94 per cent accuracy. This experience made Stander try a more scientific study (Stander et al. 1997) of the accuracy of the Bushmen. An adult male zebra that had died of anthrax was then fed upon by a pride of lions, followed by spotted hyenas and vultures. Bushmen brought to the site reconstructed what had happened from the spoor. They were able to tell that the lions did not kill the zebra and could tell the sequence of the animals who later fed on the carcass. Stander measured the tracks of the different animals and was able to show that the Bushmen were correct that each animal had its own individual way of walking, which the trackers used to reconstruct the events:

> Irregularity in soil types led to considerable variation in the spoor measurement of individual animals, yet the trackers were not only capable of recognizing such variations, but also appeared to allow for them during interpretations of spoor. The team explained that they recognize different individuals by idiosyncratic variation in the size and shape of spoor ... each individual animal has a particular way of walking, regardless of the speed of locomotion. (Ibid: 339)

Tracking goes beyond simple rational observation. It enters the realm of inductive reasoning, the basis of the scientific method (Liebenberg 1990). Such skills cannot be learnt without a long period of intimacy with how tracks are made, and with the behaviour of the animals who made them (McCallum 2005). The animals are not just a source of meat, although this is the primary objective. Hunters across the globe merge with their prey; some of the Bushmen even say that they can feel the animal under their skin. To Western sensibilities this sounds a bit spiritual and New Age, but hunters remain the closest to their environments of any people living today. Domestication of plants and animals has generally meant that humans no longer can be in close contact with their environment.

111812

444411178901

Figure 3.2: Bushman hunters disguised as ostriches, water-colour by Charles Davidson Bell (Bell Trust Collection, UCT).

By ownership of land and resources they become cut off from sharing the needs of the environment, and treat it as something to be controlled, even raped. One has only to think of the photographs of the mass shooting of migratory herds of springbok in the 19th century to realise how divorced these colonial hunters were from the long-term needs and survival of a precious resource. There is a telling picture in Johnson et al. (1979: Figure 28) of a group of Bushmen sitting around a clutch of ostrich eggs. They are shaking the eggs to know which ones are fertilised and which are not. The fertilised eggs will remain on the nest, while the others will be taken back to camp to be eaten. This is awareness that one does not strip a resource (unless, of course, one is very hungry).

48

Figure 3.3: Ju/'hoansi hunter with collected bulb (Andrew Smith).

Gathering

While much of the focus on foraging people in archaeology is on the hunted component in the diet (men's work), this is primarily due to the preservation of food resources. Animal bones survive, whereas plant remains are few and far between. It is important to recognise that hunters are not always success-ful in their daily contribution to the diet. Gathering by women at times provides over 70 per cent of calories consumed (Lee 1979), although women will say they have not eaten unless there is meat available. This could have a double meaning, because meat and sex are closely linked, and a good hunter is a desirable husband. Women are also skilled botanists: the Ju/'hoansi of Nyae Nyae can identify over 200 species of plants, of which at least 105 are edible (Lee 1979: 158–159). Men will gather too, especially if no meat has been obtained, but much less often than women (Figure 3.3).

Gathering allows women to have their children close at hand. While collecting plants, they can read sign and tell their husbands what game they have seen and where this was. Plants gathered are mostly food, but women also collect useful plants (for firewood, shelter, tools, etc.) and medicinal plants. At the coast, gathering would include seafood such as shellfish, octopus, crayfish and other marine species found in the intertidal zone.

Medicine and healing

Healing rituals are performed around the trance dance among southern African hunters. Healers are not given any special place within the society, and anyone, either male or female, can become trancers, although usually it is men. To be a healer, though, is a calling that few take on because it is dangerous. Drawing sickness requires the healer to go into a trance during which he visits the spirit world and obtains the power to heal. This condition is called 'the little death' because the climax of the trance has such a powerful impact upon both body and mind. Among the Ju/'hoansi this moment is known as *kia*, which one trancer describes: 'As we enter *kia*, we fear death. We fear we may die and not come back' (Katz 1982: 45). The healer at that moment is no longer in control, and his friends have to make sure that he does not fall into the fire and hurt himself. The healing power is manifest in the healer's sweat, which is placed upon the sick person. The trancer does his utmost to pull the sickness from his patient. This is done by the laying of hands across the body. One healer, who had been trying to pull the sickness from his wife for years, said that he even pulled a little piece of metal from her legs and hips (Ibid: 110). This is not unlike Colonel Gordon's experience in December 1778 when he witnessed a healer in the Koo pull beetles out of the sore leg of a young man (Cullinan 1992: 67), while Silberbauer (1981: 176) described the G/wi Iron Dance as 'being the prelude to curative "surgery" in which foreign objects, associated with the patient's illness, are removed from his body'.

The trance dance is not just about physical healing; it can be used to heal rifts within the group. If the dispute is too great and cannot be healed by the dance, then one of the groups may decide to strike camp and go elsewhere. This fluidity underscores how camps change over the year, with people coming to visit kin or moving to a new place to hunt.

The trance dance is the most powerful healing mechanism among hunter-gatherers, but they are also fine botanists and have a good knowledge of medicinal plants, some of which might be used to assist in the healing dances. There is some magic and spirituality involved in their use, especially when eland fat is mixed with the plants (Marshall 1976).

Hunters becoming herders?

One aspect of the debate on the development of pastoralism in southern Africa has been the belief that local hunters were capable of obtaining stock through internal exchange systems, and thus became the Khoekhoen (Sadr 2003). The difficulty in achieving this, at least among the immediate-return hunters of southern Africa, is that they are strongly egalitarian, with no leaders, and an aversion to private ownership (Smith 2017). If they had wanted to become herders, these hunters had access to two herd animals that could have been eminently tractable: eland and buffalo. The hunters knew these animals intimately and could have learnt to herd them. It is not a simple matter for immediate-return hunters to become pastoralists. It is almost as if the hunters refuse the responsibility of pastoralism, perhaps because that would domesticate them too. They might take on some small stock if they have been settled around a village, but even those animals look after themselves (Yellen 1984). I was told of a case where one hunter near a village had 400 goats and people despised what they considered his arrogance. He could not marry off his daughter. When he sold off the goats, he was once more accepted and his daughter found a husband (Alison Brooks, personal communication).

An example of the difficulty of hunters taking up animal husbandry was the experiment by the first British governor at the Cape at the end of the 18th century, Lord Macartney, who attempted to stop Bushmen raiding of farmers by making the Bushmen responsible stock keepers (Penn 2005: 231). The farmers gave the hunters as many as 2 000 sheep and goats in one year, which had the desired effect of reducing the raids. In 1820, the magistrate Andries Stockenström, on a mission to find out what was happening on the frontier, noted that some Bushmen had taken up herding (Wilson 1969: 71), but the hunters mostly slaughtered the animals and ate them. Stockenström (Hutton 1887, vol I: 228) stated that the Bushmen 'are in the lowest savage state, and we shall have gained a great point if we raise them one step by making them graziers and rendering their subsistence less precarious'. He wanted to keep the colonists from expanding beyond the boundary he was then recommending. This, of course, was virtually impossible since the frontier was uncontrolled at that time. The precariousness he talked about was due not only to their land being usurped but also to the game being so severely shot out. This meant that the alternatives for the Bushmen were to steal stock to stay alive (resulting in commandos of Boers or Griquas going out and killing them) or to become virtual slaves to the stock owners. Usually what happened, though, was that the commandos would kill all the members of a kraal; if they saved the children, they brought them back to work on farms (Adhikari 2010).

CHAPTER 4

Rock Art and Symbolism

Although Later Stone Age hunter-gatherers did not have a written language, they were able to communicate spiritual ideas on the rock walls of caves. The rock art of Africa is as beautiful and as informative about the people who painted it as that found in the rest of the world, such as the cave paintings of France and Spain, or the Dreamtime paintings of Australia. This can be seen in the magnificent paintings from the Sahara (Lajoux 1963) and southern Africa (Pager 1972).

Two 18th-century travellers into the interior of South Africa recorded seeing Bushman rock paintings. When Colonel Robert Gordon, the head of the garrison at the Cape, travelled to the Seekoei River Valley (a southern tributary of the Orange/Gariep River) and the Sneeuberg Mountains, he noted in his journal for 16 November 1777: 'Here for the first time I saw their drawings on the rocks. Some were reasonable, but on the whole they were poor and exaggerated. They had painted various animals, mostly in black, also red and yellow, and some people. I could easily believe that it has been said they painted animals unknown to man, since in many cases

Figure 4.1: Copy of Bushman paintings by Colonel Robert
Jacob Gordon, Sneeuberg Mountains (Gordon Archive,
Rijksmuseum, Amsterdam).

one had to guess what they were. I made drawings of the best
ones' (Raper & Boucher 1988: 83–84). These are the first known
copies made of the rock art in southern Africa (see Figures 4.1
and 4.2).

Perhaps Gordon only saw a few examples of the rock art.
Certainly, the second traveller to comment on the art, Sir John
Barrow, travelling in the same area as Gordon in 1797, is much
more positive about those paintings he saw:

> On the smooth sides of the cavern were drawings of sev-
> eral animals that had been made from time to time by
> these savages. Many of them were caricatures; but oth-
> ers were too well executed not to arrest attention. The

Figure 4.2: Copy of Bushman paintings by Colonel Robert Jacob Gordon, Sneeuberg Mountains (Gordon Archive, Rijksmuseum, Amsterdam)

different antelopes that were there delineated had each their character so well discriminated, that the originals, from whence the representations had been taken, could, without any difficulty, be ascertained ... The force and spirit of drawings, given to them by bold touches judiciously applied, and by the effect of light and shadow, could not be expected from savages ... I had frequently heard the peasantry mention the drawings in the mountains behind the Sneuwberg [*sic*] made by the Bosjesmans; but took it for granted they were caricatures only, similar to those on the doors and walls of uninhabited buildings,

the works of idle boys; and it was no disagreeable disap-
pointment to find them very much the reverse. Some of
the drawings were known to be new; but many of them
had been remembered from the first settlement of this
part of the colony. (Barrow 1801, vol 1: 239–240)

Even if he called the artists 'savages', Barrow was among
the first Europeans to see the art as being special. Even
though there were still Bushmen painters around at the end
of the 18th century, Barrow, like his contemporaries, unfortunately was not curious enough to ask why the art had
been created. The interpretation of what the rock art means
has had to come from outside analyses, as no painters were
interviewed during the colonial period. Various theories have
been put forward to answer this question, ranging from 'art
for art's sake' (the artist just expressing himself, much like a
modern painter might do) to sympathetic magic to improve
hunting success. The large numbers of animals depicted,
particularly the eland, would seem to suggest the latter reason. Another suggestion is that the art depicted myths. This
was challenged by Stow (1905: 122), who spent many years
tracing the cave art, although not always very accurately,
especially when Victorian morality came into play and did
not allow erect penises to be shown (Dowson et al. 1994).
What is interesting is that Stow recognised the importance of
the trance dance as described by Qing, the Bushman informant and guide of Joseph Orpen (1874), and Stow believed
he could recognise it in some of the paintings he visited: '[I]t
unmistakably proves that a certain amount of religious belief
was connected with some of their dances' (Stow 1905: 121).

The importance of what Stow had recognised was not taken up for another 70 years, until Patricia Vinnicombe (1976) also made the connection between the art and trance activities. This was followed up by David Lewis-Williams (1981), who then looked at rock art more widely, even examining the cave art of France and Spain as earlier indicators of what the art might have meant to the hunters.

While there may be some argument about details, there is general consensus among scholars that the rock art is not purely descriptive. It represents deep meaning and communication at a sophisticated level (Lewis-Williams 1981). The figures, both human and animal, represent experiences of the trancer when s/he visited the land of the spirits to bring back healing power to their people. As we saw in Chapter 3, at the height of the trance the sweat of the healer is rubbed on a sick person to make them better. Since there is no separation between the 'real' world and the 'spirit' world, the rock face is interpreted as a veil in which one fuses with the other. A number of images show an animal, such as a snake, coming out of a crack in the rock, as though appearing from inside the rock face. In Western terms, could this be seen as Alice crossing over into Wonderland, or Orphée going into the Underworld through the mirror in Jean Cocteau's famous film (1950): the land of dreams? There are images of therianthropes, or animal-headed people, seen as the healer in altered states of consciousness, and becoming part animal/part human. So powerful are these beliefs that some trancers are believed to change form and even to become lions. Can you imagine how powerful the sight of a lion sleeping under a rock wall with paintings on it (Figure 4.3) might be?

Figure 4.3: Lion sleeping under a rock overhang with paintings above, Niassa National Park, Mozambique (Colleen and Keith Begg).

Entoptics

Humans going into altered states of consciousness all react the same way, no matter where they come from. It is part of the way the human brain is wired. There are three stages of altered consciousness that have been recognised by laboratory experiment (Lewis-Williams & Dowson 1989: 60–67). In the first stage, people see zig-zags, dots and whorls. In the second stage this develops into a deeper trance experience, and the subjects see and feel a world more familiar to them, and can hear water, experience thirst, etc. The third stage is the deepest, and people in deep trance talk about entering a hole in the ground and seeing 'real world' imagery of animals and people. These different stages have been recognised in the rock art: stage one with grids, zig-zags, mesh shapes (such as nets); stage two with nested 'U' shapes and buzzing (interpreted as beehives); stage three with snakes coming out of the rock face, people with animal heads, etc. This last stage accompanies visual images of trancers in the dance, which include the 'bent-over posture' assumed by the shaman when dancing, and bleeding from the nose, which would occur when the shaman was physically under stress when entering the spirit world (Figure 4.4). Interviews with shamans have reported that at the moment of the climax, the power shoots up the spine and out of the top of the head. This, among the Ju/'hoansi Bushmen of Nyae Nyae, is called *kia* (Katz 1982), as we have seen in Chapter 3.

Although the meaning of the art is deeply embedded within hunting society's belief systems, and the range of distribution, from Zimbabwe, Namibia and Botswana and all across South Africa, has recognisable common themes, it is important to recognise what Guenther (1994: 257) says: '[T]he themes of ritual and art do not touch upon many of the myths and tales that people tell one another.' Thus, the three themes of Bushman expressive culture – art, ritual and folklore – are not homogeneous. In other words, visual images could depend on local interpretations.

However, while the trance hypothesis may be the main underlying driving force, and the art is shamanistic, that is, it records the experience of the 'out-of-body' trancer bringing back healing power from the land of the spirits, there may be other metaphors in the symbolism. Anne Solomon (1995) focuses on what she calls 'mythic women', where a number of

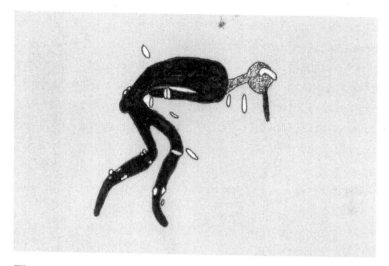

Figure 4.4: A shaman in bent-over posture, bleeding from the nose (after Lewis-Williams & Dowson 1989: 44).

images from all across southern Africa show human figures with legs spread apart and what is interpreted as fluid emanating from the body. She interprets this as menstrual or amniotic fluid, suggesting that these images may be a metaphor for the power inherent in sexual potency used in rain-making within the wider realm of gender relationships: for example, eland fat can mean sexual intercourse, rain and potency.

A third potential area of the art is the depiction of an actual event, such as the boys' puberty ritual discussed below, hunting scenes or battle scenes, all recording specific events of significant meaning to the group experiencing the event. These depictions can then be incorporated into future spiritual use by later observers.

The Drakensberg area of the Eastern Cape and KwaZulu-Natal is particularly rich in rock-art sites. A fine example is

Storm Shelter (Figure 4.5), which exhibits a wide range of images, both human and animal. The painted panel is six metres long, with 231 identifiable images, the greatest number of them human, but includes 43 eland and 32 rhebok pictures. In addition, there are many therianthropes (half human/half animal) (Blundell 2004). The overprinting of images is an excellent indication of consistent use of the shelter over time, which would have meant it was a place of power for shamans to reach into the spirit world.

Of the animal images, the depiction of eland is consistently the most common (Figure 4.5). This is because the eland is the rain animal, representing the good life that comes with the rains. Animals become fat with the new grass, and they produce offspring. Young women also produce babies, so this underlies the strong relationship between fecundity, rain and sex imbued in the eland image. In the later period this metaphor is carried over to cattle, and some cattle drawings have been found overprinted on eland (SL Hall 1986) (Figure 4.6). Were the cattle becoming rain animals? Or was this part of the increased pressure by both Bantu-speaking farmers and colonialists in the 19th century, causing changes among the hunters of the then Cape Colony?

Puberty rituals

When young Khoekhoe and Bushmen boys and girls reached puberty there were ceremonies that allowed them to move into adulthood. Among the Khoekhoe girls this was (and still is among the Nama) seclusion in a hut while being helped by

Figure 4.5: Rock panel in Storm Shelter, Drakensberg, Eastern Cape, South Africa (Andrew Smith).

Figure 4.6: Cattle image overprinted on an eland, Eastern Cape, South Africa (Andrew Smith).

an older woman (called *abu taras*) (Schapera 1930: 274). All Khoekhoe ceremonies required the slaughter of a sheep, and for a young girl this would have been a ewe. When the meat was cooked, it was eaten separately from the rest of the group.

Young boys were also initiated individually by seclusion where each was instructed how to be a man by observing moral rules. Until this happened, he could only eat with women, but after the ritual sheep was slaughtered and the men agreed he should be welcomed into their ranks, he would then be considered *doro-aob* (of age), and could sit in with the men around the fire (Schapera 1930: 283).

Khoe ceremonies were very different from initiation in Bushman society. At first menses, a young Bushman girl would be considered taboo and secluded in a small hut tended only by women until she was ready for the eland dance, when a feast was prepared for her (Ibid: 119). Boys, on the other hand, were initiated as a group in a place away from women. Their seclusion was initially a rough one, being half-starved and without meat. The day would be spent dancing in a circle, learning the mysteries of ritual belief, including trancing. An example of just such a ceremony can be seen in the rock art of Sevilla, in the Cederberg of the Western Cape, traced by Royden Yates (Yates et al. 1990: 55; Parkington & Paterson, in press). The scene seems to show naked boys in two rows, the top of which has a series of kaross-clad, bow-carrying older men immediately behind (see Figure 4.7). According to Schapera, Bushmen initiation was 'intimately connected with hunting ... Hottentot boys ... are initiated individually, and the rites do not appear to have any connection with either hunting or religious mysteries' (Schapera 1930: 284). The Sevilla rock-art initiation sequence

Figure 4.7: Boys' puberty ceremony, Sevilla, Cederberg, Western Cape (after Yates et al. 1990: Figure 29).

contradicts Schapera, who stated, in contrast to the ceremonies of northwestern Bushman groups in Namibia, 'There is no definite record of any puberty ceremonies for boys among the southern Bushmen' (Ibid: 125). The Sevilla rock art certainly seems to show that southern Bushmen did indeed have dancing rituals. There is an eland body below the activity scene, again stressing the spiritual potency, as well as pigment 'splotches' below the scene, which show indications of rubbing. Was this due to later groups interacting with the panel, and the use of this locality as a ritual space?

Symbolism

The rock art of southern Africa may have exhibited a number of metaphors for rituals. These included rain-making and healing – all part of the trance-dance symbolism in the pictures. Another interesting aspect is the dots that run down the mythical animal's back, or, as has been mentioned above, the power shooting up the shaman's spine. This is suggested as the climax of the trance when the shaman has entered the spirit world. Dots appear in lines on many rock walls (see Figure 4.3). Are these symbols of the trance? Is it possible that these dots would be interpreted by the Bushmen as metaphors for the trance, a shorthand similar to that of the cross for Christians – a symbol that needs no further explanation?

Geometric art

Bushman rock art is generally easy to recognise, as it encompasses both human and animal figures. Although these may be distorted, they can be identified as animate, as they may be trance animals of a different form. There is another art form that is made up of more crude geometric images and is not easily understood. The distribution of these images in the eastern part of South Africa, and along western river systems, has convinced Smith and Ouzman (2004) that they were done by the Khoekhoen. This art has been described as not being fine-lined like the Bushman art. It consists of 'rough-pecked and finger-painted' lines or concentric circles, and in places has been found on top of Bushman paintings, which means it is later, but is seen as 'non-entoptic', or not related to the trance symbolism of the Bushman art.

If, indeed, the art was painted by the Khoekhoen, it would mean a date of less than 2 000 years ago. Smith and Ouzman suggest it was done in the first millennium AD and may even be related to the geometric art of Central Africa, brought south by the herders along with their domestic animals.

Conclusion

The awareness that rock art goes far beyond the purely pictorial is an important step in our understanding of the belief system of the Bushmen. At the time a painting was executed, demonstrating the experience of a shaman's having visited the spirit world, it would most likely have been part of the trance dance. The repeated overprinting tells us that this activity happened over considerable periods of time, with succeeding generations using the spiritual power of a place to draw upon healing. The skill of the artists also indicates that painting may well have been part of the training of a shaman and would probably have taken some time to achieve. To interact with the rock surface could have been dangerous if the painter was not experienced in both trancing and painting.

We still have to learn the meaning of the Khoekhoen geometric art. If the researchers are correct that it is not entoptic, then it would not have been used the same way as the hunter art for trance symbolism. It was still a means of communication and may also have been used for ritual purposes.

CHAPTER 5

Khoekhoen and the Development of Herding in Africa

The Khoekhoen should be considered as another example of traditional African herders, similar to the Nuer of Sudan (Evans-Pritchard 1940) or the Maasai of Kenya and Tanzania (Spear & Waller 1993). All domestic animals of Africa, with the exception of the donkey, came from the Near East, and there is a direct connection between the animals of North Africa and those of southern Africa.

Around 8 000 years ago, the first domestic animals arrived in North Africa. They spread throughout the Sahara, and the herders lovingly depicted their animals on the rock walls of caves (Lajoux 1963). We know that these animals were very important to them because each animal is painted showing the different coat colours. The conditions in the Sahara at that time were very favourable for keeping livestock. The rainfall belts that provide the necessary moisture for good grazing penetrated deeper into the continent, from both the North Atlantic and the Inter-Tropical Convergence Zone (ITCZ), which comes from the Gulf of Guinea. This meant that the desert was minimal, with the Sahel Zone, the southern fringe of the Sahara, at least 250 kilometres north of where it is today. Pastoral sites from this period have been found all across the Sahara (Di Lernia 1999; Smith 2008).

Around 4500 years ago the ITCZ retreated and the Sahara started to dry up. The pasture and lakes disappeared, making life harder for both the people and their animals. The southward movement of the ITCZ also meant the retreat of the tsetse-fly belts that had existed south of the Sahara. These had prevented earlier occupation by herders, as trypano-somiasis (sleeping sickness, carried by the tsetse fly) is fatal to cattle. A tsetse-free corridor to Kenya probably existed either through the Ethiopian highlands (tsetse are sensitive to altitude) or along the east coast. This offered a route of escape southwards from the drying desert. Domestic animals moved south towards East Africa, arriving before 4000 BP (Before Present, a convenient way of expressing radiocarbon dating) (Marshall 2000).

In took another thousand years for domestic animals to spread widely towards the south across the grasslands of Kenya and Tanzania. This was probably due to the herders and their animals' needing time to adjust to a new environment that harboured a number of epizootic diseases prevalent in East Africa that are fatal to cattle. These include not only sleeping sickness but also East Coast fever and malignant catarrhal fever, the latter transmitted from newborn wilde-beest. The herders learnt which areas to avoid at the appro-priate season (Gifford-Gonzalez 2000). Wright (2013), on the basis of his excavations in the lowland area of Kenya, says that the climatic conditions for the spread of herding between 4000 and 3000 BP may also not have been very favourable, inhibiting easy adjustment to this new environment by people with domestic animals. Following this, Gifford-Gonzalez (2016) revisited her data, and came to the same conclusion she had 15 years earlier: that incoming pastoralists needed time to learn about disease vectors in East Africa. An early date of 3500 BP has been recorded in northern Tanzania (Seitsonen 2012), indicating how far the herders were trying to push their grazing areas while they were learning about these diseases.

In East Africa today, herders show a respect for their animals similar to that seen in the rock art further north. Among the Nuer each coat colour has a different name (Evans-Pritchard 1940: Figure 9), and young men who get an animal from their father, as part of their initiation, will sing to that animal. This same distinction is also found in Uganda among the Karimojong, with each coat colour being distinguished (Dyson-Hudson 1966: Figure 16), and a herder will have a mental map of his herd that can immediately tell him if an animal is missing.

Animal bones excavated in the area to the east of Lake Victoria had a C4 isotope signature, which would indicate a grassland environment and thus a poor area for tsetse (Chritz et al. 2015). This offered a connection with the northern end of the tsetse-free corridor linking Tanzania and Zambia with the northern Kalahari (Figure 5.1). Around 2000 years ago, domestic animals arrived in southern Africa from East Africa, probably using this tsetse-free corridor. Mixed herds of cattle and sheep have been identified in the northern Kalahari at this time (Robbins et al. 2008), but it would appear that it was mostly sheep that continued to expand southwards, as few

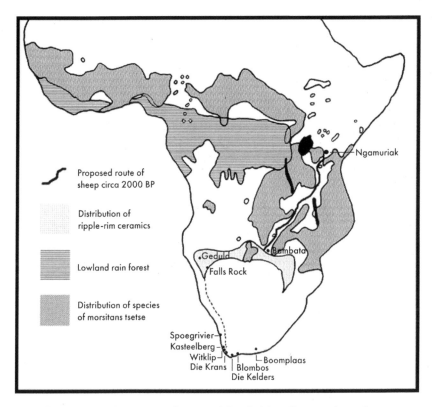

Figure 5.1: The tsetse-free corridor linking East and southern Africa, and the distribution of 'ripple-rim' (thin-walled) ceramics across the northern Kalahari (Andrew Smith).

cattle bones from the first millennium have been found in the southwestern Cape.

In the southeastern parts of South Africa, Early Iron Age farmers arrived around 1600 years ago bringing herds of cattle with them. These people's herds were probably quite small, as the environment only became amenable to larger herds by the time of the Later Iron Age (around 1000 BP), once the farmers had removed some of the bush vegetation that would have supported tsetse (M Hall 1986). Today, the Zulu have a relationship with their herds that is similar to the East African herders, and the coat colour of each animal has a different name, which is described in poetic terms (Poland et al. 2000). It is possible that these Later Iron Age Nguni-speakers were the source of the cattle seen among the Khoekhoen by the first Portuguese visitors at the end of the 15th century.

Our knowledge of the historic Khoekhoen mostly comes from the earliest Dutch colonists in the 17th and 18th centuries. By the end of the 18th century there were few independent Khoe herders. Their livestock had either been traded for non-productive items (such as alcohol) or stolen by the colonists. The last groups at this time lived in Namaqualand, where Colonel Robert Gordon met them (Raper & Boucher 1988), and were called Namaqua. Their descendants still live in the Northern Cape and Namibia, and still speak Nama, the last surviving remnant of the Khoekhoe language.

Because their animals needed pasture and water, and these might not be available everywhere, African pastoralists such as the Khoekhoen had to move around. This lifestyle is called 'transhumance', and means that their tools and other goods had to be light and portable, being mostly made of wood or leather (Figure 5.2). The Khoekhoen had portable mat houses called *matjieshuise*, which were made from saplings dug into the ground and bent over so they could be tied at the top. This framework was then covered by woven mats (see Figure 7.6), which could be carried on their oxen when the people moved camp.

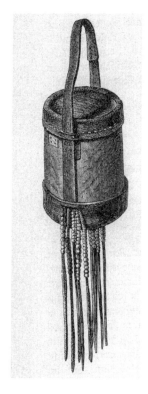

Figure 5.2: Namaqua box for holding fat (probably for coating the body), made of wood and leather (Rakel 1894: 702).

The Western Cape, and the country north to Namibia, is a winter-rainfall area. This was one reason that Bantu-speaking people only came to the Cape after the colony was set up. They had summer-rainfall crops that could not do well in the Cape. The Khoekhoen did not grow crops, although some observers said they grew dagga, but this could have been traded (for discussion, see Elphick 1985: 65–67). Some visitors, such as John Davys aboard the *Lion* (1598), saw them burn the veld (Raven-Hart 1967: 20), probably to stimulate young grass growth for their animals.

Transhumance was the reason that the Khoekhoen left

the Cape for the interior on a seasonal basis, and why the
Dutch were not able to trade for animals during their first
months following their arrival in 1652 (Thom 1952).

Origins of Khoekhoen

Where Khoekhoen came from has been a subject of lively
debate since the 18th century. It was originally thought that
they were physically and linguistically similar to herding
people from North Africa, called Hamites (after Ham, one
of Noah's sons in the Bible). The linguistic connection was
disproven by Maingard in 1934, although Westphal (1963)
showed that the language of the Cape Khoekhoen was
similar to that spoken in northern Botswana. Subsequent linguistic work by Güldemann (2008) has confirmed this, and
the Khoe-Kwadi group is seen as the progenitor.

The archaeology of herding societies in southern Africa
relies primarily on the dispersal of sheep. The earliest sheep
remains have been found at Toteng in Botswana, dated to before 2000 BP (Robbins et al. 2008), as well as at Spoegrivier
Cave in Namaqualand, at 2100 BP (Webley 2001), and at
Blombos Cave on the South Coast from around 2000 BP
(Henshilwood 1996).

Human genetic evidence also has a role to play, as we will
see in Chapter 8. Y-chromosome (male) data shows a connection between East and southern Africa (Henn et al. 2008).
Another link can be seen in the gene marker -14010G>C,
known as lactase persistence, which allows those who have it
to metabolise fresh milk. This is suggested as being derived

from East African pastoralists, and is also found in southern Africa (Breton et al. 2014). Interesting, however, is the limited mtDNA (female) connection between East and southern Africa. This hints at East African males coming into southern Africa, and probably taking local wives. The linguistic data would support this, as there is evidence of substrates (mutual grammatical elements) from Bushman languages in Khoekhoe (Güldemann 2008; see Figure 8.1).

Becoming Khoekhoen

From available dating, the arrival of domestic animals in southern Africa began when the Kalahari experienced a wetter period conducive to herding after 2 500 years ago. As mentioned above, sheep remains have been identified in the northern Kalahari, down the west coast of Namaqualand and on to the Western Cape from around 2 000 years ago, indicating a rapid movement down the Atlantic West Coast. One possible trigger for the southward movement of stock was increasing social and economic complexity in East Africa around 3000 BP, as a result of Bantu-speaking farmers coming around the northern edge of the tropical forest from the Cross Rivers area of Cameroon, as well as Cushitic-speaking farmers from Ethiopia and herders escaping the drier conditions of the Sahara, all arriving in an area already occupied by hunters. This could have created a bow wave of herders looking for new pastures to the south, ahead of later Bantu-speaking migrants.

The debate on the spread of herding societies in South Africa initially revolved around two competing theories:

1. As Sadr (1998, 2005; Sadr & Sampson 2006) was unable to connect pottery styles across southern Africa, he has suggested that stock were transferred between hunting bands by internal exchange mechanisms (such as *xharo*, used by modern Ju/'hoansi Bushmen), from which grew fully fledged herding societies.

2. A more orthodox version propounded by Smith (2006) suggests that stock were accompanied by immigrant herders who possibly spoke a Khoe language, which had East African antecedents.

There has been some concession on Sadr's (2018) part, and even though he cannot see any changes in the stone tools or what shellfish the people preferred, a small-scale population movement may have infiltrated southern Africa, bringing ceramics with them.

There are three different strands of evidence, namely archaeology, linguistics and genetics, which we can merge into a single model to explain the spread of domestic stock to southern Africa. Each strand, it must be recognised, is based on an independent and mutually exclusive database. To correlate such diversity requires being able to anchor an event with dates that can be verified within a narrow time frame. In archaeology this is usually dependent on radiocarbon dates that have a low 2 sigma (usually written as ±25–40 years BP). We prefer not to use genetic dating, as this may measure divergence of haplogroups (different genetic groups), and although dates derived this way may have relative value, they are too crude to be used when not calibrated against radiocarbon dates. Equally, they cannot tell us about the adaptive significance or why such events occurred. Similarly, the debate on glottochronology (the study of chronological relationships between languages) has rejected any fixed date for linguistic divergence, and what this might mean. By the same token, archaeological modelling is not able to say anything fixed about genetic or linguistic diversity.

Domestic animals arrived in southern Africa from further north, presumably East Africa. Genetic studies of sheep remains from South Africa indicate a Near Eastern source, confirmed by analyses of modern breeds (Mugai et al. 2004). Two varieties are known: thin-tailed and fat-tailed. The thin-tailed probably came from the Levant along with cattle sometime after 8000 BP. The fat-tailed would seem to have come via the Yemen, as those of East Africa are closely related to the Mahli of the Arabian Peninsula (Mugai & Hanotte 2013). The indigenous thin-tailed (Figure 5.3) and fat-tailed (Figure 5.4) breeds were depicted by early travellers in South Africa during the 18th century. Both breeds were noted for being hairy and long-legged. Fat-tailed sheep were depicted in the rock art of the Cape Mountains.

Before the second millennium AD, or 1 000 years ago, cattle numbers in southern Africa were probably very small, as sheep dominated the domestic herds. As we have noted, these animals arrived with pastoralists 2 000 years ago. Around 1 800 years ago, the first Early Iron Age farmers came south, also bringing some cattle and small stock. Initially, the caprines were mostly sheep rather than goats, and the small stock was more numerous than cattle, at least until the 8th century. The concept of the Central Cattle Pattern, with a circle of huts around a cattle byre in the middle, existed with the Early Iron

Figure 5.3: Thin-tailed sheep, 18th-century colour sketch by Colonel Robert Jacob Gordon (Gordon Archive, Rijksmuseum, Amsterdam).

Age, but the cattle herds were probably much more restricted than in the Later Iron Age when the homestead types became much more varied (Mitchell 2002: Chapter 12). The number of goats also increased at this time, as goats were most probably better accustomed to the more sedentary life around farms (Badenhorst 2018). Cattle appear in large numbers with the arrival of the Later Iron Age Nguni-speakers (direct ancestors of the modern Zulu and Xhosa in the eastern part of South Africa, or even Sotho-Tswana speakers further north).

This is the same time that increased cattle herds seem to have arrived into Khoekhoe society. We have to ask: is this a

Figure 5.4: Fat-tailed sheep, illustration by Samuel Daniel, 1806 (Andrew Smith).

coincidence? I don't believe so, and because there existed Khoe/Xhosa mixed groups (such as the Gonaqua) in the Eastern Cape, there is a good chance that this could have been the route of arrival of cattle as an economic and sociable mainstream of herding society further west in the winter-rainfall area of the Cape. Support for this comes from isotopic analysis done by Judy Sealy (2010) on human skeletons along the south coast of South Africa. At the beginning of the second millennium AD there was a marked shift away from C3 isotopes, which would come from eating the meat of browsing wild animals, to C4, interpreted as people eating more food derived from C4 grazers. This was probably milk obtained from increased cattle numbers (or bulk grazers) appearing along the coast. Other support for the late arrival of cattle into the Western and Southern Cape comes from a study by Horsburgh and Gosling (2020). Because of the difficulty osteologists often have in separating the species of large bovid bones (such as cattle and eland), ancient DNA (aDNA) was used on samples of bone that would have fallen within the known size of cattle from four different sites dating to the first millennium AD. The researchers failed to find any cattle bones in their sample. All were either eland, buffalo or gemsbok. Their sample of 20 bones was quite small, but it does indicate the probability of low numbers of cattle to be found at the Cape before 1 000 years ago.

Elphick (1985) argues that the Khoekhoen introduced herding to the Nguni, and the Khoe, having come from the east, gave the 'Chobona' the honour of being the recognised hierarchical rulers. This may be true as far as the development of Nguni-speakers in the Eastern Cape is concerned, but although the Chobona may have been recognised as leaders, this may only have been the result of their wealth in cattle, before these animals were transferred to the west.

Regardless of the history of these relationships, there can be no doubt that with the arrival of the large cattle herds seen among the historic Khoekhoen, this would have increased their status against the hunters, or Soaqua, compared with what had existed previously with sheep herding. The hunters would have been increasingly marginalised at the bottom of the social hierarchy, and, when first seen by the Dutch colonists of the 17th century, were described as working for Khoe or as cattle thieves.

Pottery

Pottery was well-established among Kansyore hunter-fisher-shellfish collectors of East Africa before 3000 BP (Dale & Ashley 2010). It included a rocker-stamped design found further north in the Nile Valley of Egypt and Sudan, from where it might have originated. Early pottery was found in the Machili and Zambezi river valleys of Zambia by 2400 BP (Phillipson 1989). It was found at two sites in the Erongo Mountains of northern Namibia: from Leopard Cave between 2400 and 2200 BP (Pleurdeau et al. 2012), and from Big Elephant Shelter (including some with spouts) between 2600 and 2550 BP (Wadley 1976). In the Namib Desert, at Snake Rock and Falls Rock around 2100–1640 BP (Kinahan 2016), and at Geduld around 2000 BP, thin-walled, black-burnished 'ripple-rim' ware was found (Smith & Jacobson 1995). This latter pottery type extends over a large area, as seen in Figure 5.1. In spite of the early radiocarbon dates, the dating of the arrival of pottery in Namibia is not conclusive. Albrecht et al. (2001) have dates of 3100 BP, but, like the two Erongo sites above, this was rejected because it did not fit with the paradigm of the moment, which said pottery only arrived with domestic stock around 2000 BP.

What was the connection further south? Could there have been an earlier migration of shellfish collectors from East Africa that was connected to those of the Western Cape between 3000 and 2000 BP? Rocker-stamped designed pottery has been found in the upper Seekoei River Valley, but came from the upper part of the sequence in two rock shelters, and the dates suggested are only 300 years ago (Sampson 1988).

There is a problem with the earliest pottery from the mega-middens of the early period. First, the pottery is assumed only to be 2 000 years old. Second, some was found quite deep in the excavations, so was assumed to have been trampled down. Third, these are only tiny fragments and so are very difficult to assign to a specific pottery type. We have to recognise that the earliest groups coming from East Africa may well have been small, and mostly males, bringing few pots with them.

A distinction has been made regarding the wall thickness of pottery before and after the arrival of Early Iron Age farmers. The earliest pottery associated with the first herders is 'thin-walled' (less than ten millimetres thick). Early Iron Age pottery is 'thick-walled' (greater than ten millimetres) (Sadr & Sampson 2006). Contrary to Sadr and Sampson's (2006: 245) assertion that no thin-walled pottery exists north of the Zambezi, it does exist in East African Kansyore ware (Ashley & Grillo 2015), in the pastoral Elmenteitan from Ngamuriak, Kenya (Robertshaw 1990), and in Narosura pottery from the Ufana Valley area, Tanzania (Prendergast et al. 2013; Grillo et al. 2018). In all cases the pottery thickness is between seven and nine millimetres. Thin-walled pottery, known as Bambata, has also been found in Zimbabwe (Walker 1983). The 'ripple-rim' ware, also thin-walled, occurs all the way across to Limpopo (Sadr 2015), the Soutpansberg (Hall & Smith 2000) and the Waterberg (Mari van der Ryst, personal communication) (see Figure 5.1), where rock paintings of sheep are also found (Eastwood & Fish 1996). Pre-Early Iron Age, thin-walled pottery was also found in KwaZulu-Natal (Mazel 1992). Analysis of residues in potsherds from two sites in highland Lesotho, Likoaeng and Sehonghong, dated to the

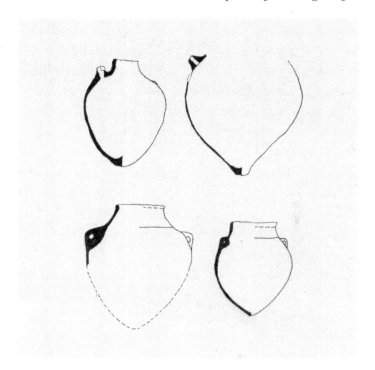

Figure 5.5: Changes in pottery, from spouted to lugged wares, in the Western Cape (based on Rudner's drawings, published in Rudner 1968: Figures VI and VII).

first millennium AD, show that milk was being used (Fewlass et al. 2020). These thin-walled ceramics, from sites ostensibly occupied by hunter-gatherers (Mitchell 1996), are not Iron Age, and are even called 'hunter-gatherer' pottery. The milk would probably have come from Early Iron Age herds in the lowlands, but it begs the following questions: where did the thin-walled pottery originate, and how was the milk metabolised by hunters who were lactose-intolerant?

At the bottom of the pottery sequence at the Cape is undecorated, black-burnished ware, dated to circa 2000 BP at Die Kelders (Schweitzer 1979). This is followed, further up the sequence, by spouted wares. Spouted pottery is also the bottom of the pastoral sequence at Kasteelberg, on the Vredenburg Peninsula (circa 1800 BP), to be replaced by lugged wares after 1000 BP (Sadr & Smith 1991). These incorporated projections with holes through them (lugs) on the shoulders to allow them to be supported or carried. Lugged ware was the characteristic pottery type of the historic Khoekhoen (Figure 5.5).

In 1721, Johann Büttner described an interesting method of firing pots (Nienaber & Raven-Hart 1970). The pots were made by women who fired them in kilns they constructed themselves. These kilns were fabricated by digging a deep hole into a steep-walled river bank. The women would light a strong fire in the hole until the interior became hard and dry after several days. The prepared pots were then put inside and fired.

The uses of pottery

We can assume that having pots made working and cooking with liquids much easier. But analysis of the residues found inside some pottery fragments from the Kasteelberg 'B' site (KBB) reveals traces of marine mammal fats rather than milk use, unlike the example of the pot residues from highland Lesotho above (Patrick et al. 1985). A similar study of pot-sherds from East Africa (Grillo et al. 2020) shows that most of the sherds with lipids came from processing meat, bones, marrow and fat. A few sherds did show milk residues, but these

stone bowls in Zambia, Namibia, Botswana and the Northern Cape of South Africa (Mitchell 2002). These are common
on Nderit pastoral sites in East Africa (Phillipson 1993). The
problem is that none of the southern African examples have a
decent archaeological context, and so there are no dates available. Because of their limited numbers, there is a good chance
that the bowls came from the outside.

The migration of Iron Age farmers

The story of migration during the African Iron Age starts with
Saharan pastoralists. They harvested wild grains as part of
their seasonal round (Smith 1980), including *Pennisetum glaucum*
(pearl millet), as seen in the large number of grindstones
found at Adrar Bous, Niger, dated between 5400 and 4100 BP
(Crader 2008). With the drying up of the Sahara after 5000
BP, groups of people in the Sahel, at the southern edge of the
Sahara, began to control their wild grain stands, leading to the
establishment of villages around them, and ultimately to the
domestication of millet. The earliest domestication of millet
was found by Manning et al. (2011), dated to around 4500 BP.
Millet spread southwards through the savannah zones of West
Africa, being taken up by farmers, such as the Kintampo in
Ghana, and continued on to Cameroon, where Neumann et
al. (2012) have dated it to between 2400 and 2200 BP.

Cameroon is the original homeland of Bantu-speaking
farmers. These were iron-using people who were able to use
their metal tools to prepare the land for swidden (moving) agriculture. This permitted their migration with pearl millet

87

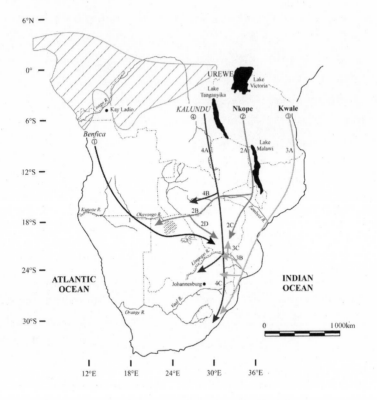

Figure 5.6: Iron Age migrations (from Huffman 2021: Figure 4; used with permission).

across the northern edge of the tropical forest to East Africa by 3000 BP, where they are known as Urewe. They also moved southward along the western edge of the forest to northern Angola, then southeastwards to northern Botswana (Denbow 1990). They did not stop there, but continued onwards towards the southeastern coast of what is now KwaZulu-Natal. This is referred to by archaeologists as Benfica, merging with the Kalundu Western Stream (Figure 5.6). On the southeastern

88

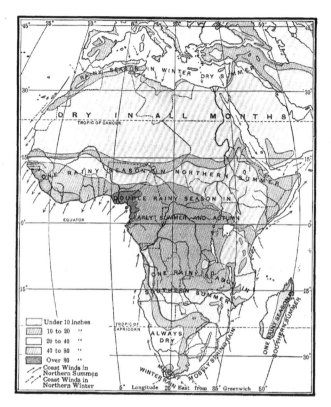

Figure 5.7: Rainfall map of Africa, originally published in 1920 (public domain).

coast they met other Iron Age farmers moving southward from East Africa, known as the Eastern Stream, or the Kwale and Nkope Traditions, around 1600 BP (Huffman 2021).

As we saw above, the first immigrants with domestic animals brought their thin-walled pottery down the tsetse-free corridor from East Africa into the Kalahari. The presence of thin-walled pottery suggests they went on to Limpopo Province and the highveld of South Africa, then to KwaZulu-Natal

89

by 2000 BP (Figure 5.1). Their pottery, however, was replaced by much thicker ceramics in the southeast once the Iron Age people had arrived.

If we compare Huffman's map (Figure 5.6) with the rainfall map of Africa (Figure 5.7), we can see that the Iron Age farmers stayed close to the southern edges of the summer-rainfall pattern as they migrated towards the southeast. This was due to their millet being a summer-rainfall crop. The southwest was a winter-rainfall area, and this was left to the Khoisan.

Kasteelberg has the seal of approval

As already inferred above, the most important herding sites so far found in the Western Cape are on Kasteelberg, a granite kopje situated about four kilometres east of Paternoster on the West Coast (Figure 5.8). The hill contains numerous sites, designated A, B, C, etc. (Sadr 2004; 2007; 2018; Smith 2006). There is evidence of Middle Stone Age occupation, but most of the sites are from Late Holocene hunter-gatherers and more recent herders. In order of excavation, the sites are: KBA, on top of the hill (1810–100 BP); KBB, at the bottom of the hill (1300–190 BP); KBC, a rock shelter close to KBA (2100–1200 BP, although there was an older date of 28 000, which would have referred to the Middle Stone Age); KBD (700 BP); and KBG (4000–1300 BP). Sadr (2018) argues that the top of the hill is just one large site that was used as an aggregation place for 'feasting'. This is a common practice among mobile herders, as mentioned above, who come together during the wet season, a time when they can stay in one place for a period of time when pasture and water are at their best (Smith 1980).

Since there was some question about when the first pastoral occupation of South Africa occurred, Sealy and Yates (1994) ran some dates on sheep bones from KBA. Their results, from the same square where the charcoal radiocarbon date of 1810 BP came, were 1630 and 1430 BP. From this they argued that sheep were not in South Africa before 1600 years ago. In an attempt to narrow down the herder occupation period of KBB, Sadr et al. (2017) added 25 new dates to the original 11 obtained during the excavations (Smith 2006). At first glance, in reading the Sadr et al. article, it looked like the dates for the occupation of KBB were the same as those for KBA. Closer examination, however, showed that the new dates were not calibrated using the marine reservoir coefficient of -146 years. In addition, further probability calibration resulted in an occupation period of 1180–740 BP. These dates confirmed what we already knew about the occupation of KBB from the excavation dates (1300–880 BP), and that KBA was occupied before KBB.

An interesting feature of this additional dating of KBB showed two periods of occupation, with a hiatus of 150 years around AD 1000. Why this gap should have occurred is not known, although it has been suggested that this was during a warming period, meaning that conditions would have been considerably drier in the winter-rainfall area. The herders may have been forced to move at this time. During this hiatus, pottery changed from spouted to lugged wares (Sadr & Smith 1991). We now know from the further dating of sheep bones from Blombos (Henshilwood 1996) that the herders were in the Western Cape of South Africa around 2000 BP.

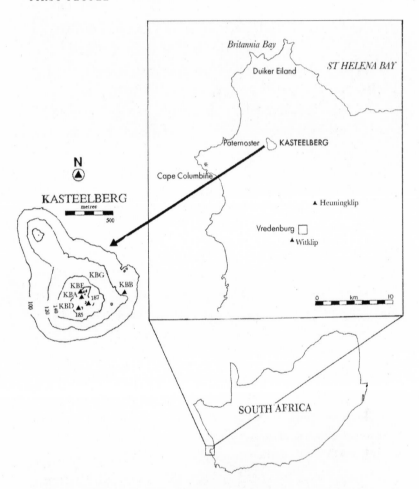

Figure 5.8: Site of Kasteelberg on the Vredenburg Peninsula, Western Cape (Andrew Smith).

Why would there have been a change in pottery styles over the 150 years of the hiatus at Kasteelberg after 1000 BP? We can assume it was a general decision, as lugged pottery is widespread across the Western Cape. There must have been a

Figure 5.9: Excavated Kasteelberg sites (Andrew Smith).

reason why spouts (for pouring?) became less important than lugs (for carrying or suspension?). Since this change also coincided with the shift to cattle pastoralism, perhaps the carrying idea meant easier transportation on the backs of cattle.

The fauna from **KBC** shows a transition from the hunting of small buck to the herding of sheep. After 1800 BP sheep comprise a good proportion of the bones found (Klein & Cruz-Uribe 1989), with very few cattle. The ratio of sheep to cattle among individual bones excavated is 548:1.

During the herding period, while sheep may have been the most important domestic animal at KBB, they only produced 27 per cent of the actual bones excavated. The animal providing the greatest total was the Cape fur seal

Figure 5.10: Excavation of Kasteelberg 'A' (KBA) (Andrew Smith).

(*Arctocephalus pusillus*), with 63 per cent. The seal bones are mostly from animals that would have been around 25 kilograms in weight; thus, a man could have carried an entire seal up from the coast only four kilometres away.

Kasteelberg becomes more than just an important herding site; it encompasses the Khoekhoen trajectory of their beginnings further north in Africa. This can be seen in the burial of a young girl from KBB: F22. (In Chapter 8 we will look at the genome of the girl and how she combines both her antecedents in East Africa, and probably further north, with the link to the Luxmanda skeleton from Tanzania.) The burial site allows us to create a picture of the life of Khoekhoen herders approximately 1 300 years ago.

Figure 5.11: Bedrock grooves, Kasteelberg (Andrew Smith).

It was a sad day when they buried her. The weather could also have been grim, with strong gusts of rain from the northwest. The family had come to dig her grave, but they were reasonably sheltered by the huge boulders that are such a feature of the Kasteelberg site. This was also a good place to put up their mat shelters, since winter and spring were the lambing times, with plenty of grass from the rains.

This season of the year also allowed the herders to harvest yearling seals. These were butchered, and the meat roasted and eaten. Whole skeletons were left on the site, while the fat was rendered in clay pots. This is supported by analyses of residues inside potsherds, where evidence of marine mammal fats has been found (Patrick et al. 1985; Copley et al. 2004).

Figure 5.12: Portable grooved stone, Kasteelberg (Andrew Smith).

The fat would have been skimmed off and collected in pots, then put into skin bags or wood and skin containers (Figure 5.2), to be mixed with the ground ochre for body painting – a good sunscreen for people who spent most of the day outside. Grinding was done on the bedrock, creating grooves (Figure 5.11), or on large stones (Figure 5.12).

Women and children would go down to the beach and collect shellfish, while the men might capture seals when they were not looking after the sheep. In the lee of the large boulders the women would make pots by coiling the clay, paddling it and building up the walls to the desired height. The pots were thin-walled, and after drying would be fired in open pits or, as mentioned above, in kilns dug into steep river banks. Both broken and unfinished ostrich eggshell beads were found in the excavation, hinting that the beads were made on the

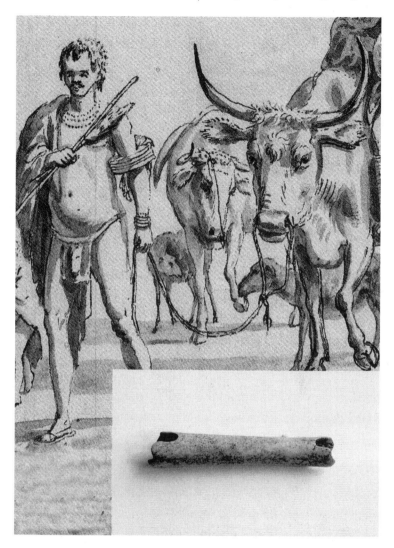

Figure 5.13: Bone found in Kasteelberg excavations, probably inserted through the nostril of an ox, as seen in this detail from a late-17th-century drawing (Smith & Pheiffer 1993: Plate 15) (inset photo of bone: Andrew Smith).

site. Men would make bone points for their arrow tips, using stone flakes. These stone tools, however, were never as good as the fine finished pieces made by the hunters from nearby Witklip.

A number of postholes were found at the bottom of KBB (Mutti 2006). These were probably the bases of mat huts (*matjieshuise*) similar to those found among the historic Khoe-khoen. In this early period of the first millennium AD, the herders only had a few cattle, possibly to use as portage animals to move their mat shelters around. These large animals were literally 'led by the nose' (Figure 5.13) by means of a rope threaded through a leg bone of a steenbok fitted into the ox's nostrils. The men would also hunt wild game when they had the chance, particularly small buck, such as steenbok or duiker. They would usually be the ones to kill a sheep, but if a woman needed to do so, perhaps for ritual purposes, she would wear a mongoose-skin cap (Smith & Pheiffer 1992: 12).

Witklip

Nine kilometres south of Kasteelberg, outside the town of Vredenburg, is the rock shelter of Witklip (Figure 5.14). This large rock provided shelter for hunters who lived in the area at the same time as the herders on Kasteelberg.

The excavation at Witklip showed that these hunters mostly had small antelope for meat, and used small stone tools as part of their hunting kit (Smith 2006). A few sheep bones and some fragments of pottery indicate they were probably in close contact with the Kasteelberg herders, and may have occasionally

Figure 5.14: Witklip, with Kasteelberg on the skyline (Andrew Smith).

been given a sheep as payment for services they provided. There were lots of wild predators, such as lion, hyena and jackal, in the area at that time, and, as noted in the historic literature, the herders often employed the hunters as guards, and to notify the stock owners of any strangers in the area who might want to steal their sheep.

CHAPTER 6

Adaptive Strategies of Khoekhoen

Among African pastoralists, transhumance is the practice of movement, often on a seasonal basis, following the pasture and water needs of their animals. This mobility means that all their worldly goods need to be portable or left in place so that they can be used when they return. The former include hut materials (mats or skins), while the latter could be grindstones, which are heavy to carry around. Because of the organic nature of their material possessions, after they have been gone for a while it is often difficult to see where they camped, especially if they were only on site for a short period of time. This has meant that the Khoekhoen have left a limited archaeological presence, and if the sites were in areas that are now ploughed fields it is very hard to find where they lived. Often the only signs of their passing might be isolated pottery sherds, as seen in the Bontebok National Park (Arthur 2008), or some traces of contact with hunters, for example the sheep bones and pottery at Witklip near Kasteelberg, as mentioned previously (Smith 2006), or even some pieces of colonial ware at KFS 5 on the Vredenburg Peninsula (Fauvelle-Aymar et al.

2006). The problem is so acute that almost no sites that can be recognised as Khoekhoen have been found in the early contact period after AD 1500. Domestic-animal remains from local animals in this period all come from colonial sites, such as Oudepost 1, on the Churchhaven Peninsula (Schrire & Deacon 1989), or the original redoubt built by the Dutch at Table Bay in the 17th century, now under the Grand Parade in Cape Town (Abrahams 1993).

Territories and land use

All nomadic people have spaces they occupy from which they obtain the resources they need for survival throughout the year. Herding people are particularly sensitive to the needs of their animals, so water and pasture would be the minimum pastoral requirements. Nomads, however, may use a territory for a period of time, but are always putting pressure on the boundaries of their territories, and so potentially are in conflict with neighbouring groups. Raiding other groups is a common practice, and this defines power between groups. The result of this is that the borders of nomadic space are never fixed and will shift over time.

When the Dutch set up their refreshment station at Table Bay in 1652 they were able to describe where various Khoe groups were to be found. This was a particular moment in pastoral time, and we can assume, given the enmity observed between groups, that their territories would have changed as one group grew stronger and put pressure on others. A sign of this was when the 'Real Saldanhars', the Cochoqua, first

101

Figure 6.1: Khoekhoe family on the move, late-17th-century drawing, National Library of South Africa (Smith & Pheiffer 1993: Plate 15).

seen between Saldanha Bay and the mountains along the Berg River to the east, came to Table Bay in 1654 to trade with the Dutch, pushing the local Peninsular Khoe aside in the process.

The transhumance between coast and interior was the reason why some European visitors to Saldanha Bay were able to trade for domestic stock, while others who came in a different season never saw a domestic animal. Herders migrated from the coast inland, probably towards the pastures around the Berg River. This information has been used to create a seasonal migration model for pastoralism in the Western Cape (Smith 1984). Thus, it would have been for the years after 1000 BP when the herds would have been cattle, bulk grazers needing to be on the move frequently to maintain the herds. Work done on isotopes from sheep teeth excavated at Kasteelberg from the previous millennium showed, however, that the flocks of sheep that could utilise local pastures did not have to travel nearly as far inland as the cattle herds, which needed larger grazing areas (Balasse et al. 2002).

As we have seen, the Khoekhoe hut (*matjieshuis*) was a simple structure. The dome-shaped hut was covered in reed mats in a specific order. To move camp, the mats were rolled up and put on the backs of oxen. The advantage of a mat house was that in summer the wind could blow through the structure, keeping it cool inside. When it rained, the mats would swell, and little rain could penetrate. As seen in Figure 6.1, the oxen were also used for riding, and there is even a record of a number of animals in a herd being used as 'war oxen', as a first line of defence, or when raiding took place (Fauvelle-Aymar 2008).

Figure 6.1 also depicts a dog. Dogs were historically seen around both Khoekhoen and Bushman huts. They were used for hunting and as a means of keeping wild animals away, as well as to alert the owners to the presence of strangers nearby. As described by Schapera (1930: 135): 'They are lean, hungry-looking mongrels, half-starved and savage-tempered.' When I visited a Ju/'hoansi village in Nyae Nyae, Namibia, the dogs I saw were just skin and bone. I hung a small skin bag I had been given on a branch outside my tent one night. By morning all that remained of it were a few fragments of hair. The dogs had eaten it.

The time when dogs arrived in southern Africa has yet to be fully determined. Mitchell (2014), using available information, suggests that they probably also came with the herders. There has been some confusion, archaeologically, as there is difficulty in separating the bones of dogs from those of jackals, and a reliable genomic study still has to be done on bones from archaeological sites to determine the earliest arrival of dogs, and with whom.

Diet

Pastoralists usually have a high milk intake, one of the main reasons to have domestic animals. Obviously, they eat meat, but small stock is the main source. In fact, Khoekhoe rituals revolved around sheep, which suggests that sheep flocks were the dominant animal in the past. Cattle were usually only eaten when an animal died. In the first millennium AD sheep dominated the faunal list at Kasteelberg, with very few cattle bones being found. Isotopic work done on sheep teeth from this period showed that there were probably two breeding periods during the year (Balasse et al. 2003). If this, indeed, was the case, then it is probable that ewe's milk was important, at least for children and women. Milk was usually drunk fresh, or it was soured. It could also be made into butter, which was eaten or used for body decoration mixed with red ochre (Schapera 1930: 237). It is important to recognise that herders had the genetic ability to metabolise raw milk, with the marker gene

-14010*C. This ability was lacking in southern African hunters (Macholdt et al. 2014).

In addition, archaeological sites from herders at the Cape show that they also hunted wild game. This is in contrast to some East African herders who do not eat wild animals, possibly because wild animals, such as young wildebeest, carry infections dangerous to cattle, so this may be a way to avoid contamination of their herds. When herders were at the coast, they ate seafood. The site of Kasteelberg (Chapter 5) is a shell midden, with large numbers of seal bones (Smith 2006) and grinding stones with ochre staining. People ate the seal meat and also mixed seal fat with red pigment as body adornment. There are historical records of butter fat also being used, and a rich man would be seen with the butter dripping off his body, a sign that he had so many cattle he could afford to waste butter.

Underground plant foods could also be used in season. In 1654, Johan Nieuhof, an early visitor to the Cape, stated that the main food of the Khoe was a kind of root, possibly *Watsonia*, 'boiled or roasted and eaten very greedily' (Raven-Hart 1971: 17).

Health

Traditional African pastoralists live reasonably healthy lives. Their groups are small, and movement means there is far less chance of pathogens that we know from agricultural and urban societies developing, such as tuberculosis or influenza.

The Khoekhoen were probably equally healthy. They

had a good diet from milk and were affected by few diseases until the smallpox epidemic arrived at the Cape in 1713. The disease was brought in on infected linen from a passing ship, afflicting the Khoekhoen in large numbers (Elphick 1985: 232). But even the impact of the 1713 epidemic may have been vastly overstated. There is good reason to think that only a maximum of 30 per cent of the population was infected (Smith 1989). Yes, this is a high number, but as a result the Khoe thought they were being bewitched and many headed away from the Cape. The combination of death and this movement resulted in fewer Khoe around Table Bay, so probably gave the impression of devastation of the population far beyond the actual effects.

The Khoekhoen had a rich pharmacopoeia that later colonists learnt to use to their advantage. For minor ailments, the Cape Khoekhoen used a wide range of local fynbos plants from which to get medical help. The Appendix to this book includes a report published in the newspaper *Het Volksblad* in 1885 listing 33 plants used by the Genadendal community. Four of these were probably of foreign origin but grew on the mission station's lands. The rest would have been traditional medicines known to the local Khoekhoen and still used by the congregation at the end of the 19th century. In the Richtersveld, the northwest corner of South Africa, at the mouth of the Orange/Gariep River, Archer (1994) was able to get information on 61 wild plants (38 above-surface, and 23 subsurface) that are considered edible (see Appendix). A total of 23 plants are still used for medicinal purposes (Archer 1994). The main season of abundance is between June and October.

Home economics, Khoekhoe style

Generally speaking, economic activities were broken down by gender and age. Men herded the animals and hunted, and women foraged for plants and small meat packages. This, however, is too crude a summary. Women did spend a lot of time at camp, and a woman owned her own hut and the space where she put the ashes from her cooking fire (Smith & Webley 2000) (see Chapter 7 on huts). There were immediate milk needs around the camp, so a small flock of ewes and a milch herd of cattle may have been kept close by. This herd was looked after by the women and children. Little boys learnt to be very skilful with animals at a young age. Girls could also help with very young animals and would also look after their younger siblings, relieving their mothers for other chores. Thus, there was an important place for everyone in the family, and each person contributed to the work that needed to be done. Khoekhoen women were skilled mat makers, making the mat covers for their *matjieshuise*. They would also work leather to make karosses for dress. In addition to camp chores were the gathering activities, and when at the coast this would have included the collection of shellfish, and possibly anything else washed up on the shore, such as young seals.

Men looked after the bulk of the herds, especially after cattle herds increased among the Khoekhoen around 1 000 years ago. The size of the herds at any moment in time depended on skilful raiding of neighbours, and on seasonal conditions affecting pasturage. There were plenty of wild animals, too, and the faunal list from Kasteelberg (Smith 2006) included virtually all the animals in the environment. Men were also skilled at working leather and wood. Since they were nomadic people, everything had to be light and portable. As we saw in Chapter 5, pottery with lugs was developed after 1000 BP. Leather cords threaded through the lugs could have allowed pots to be carried on the backs of oxen, together with the hut mats, when moving to a new site.

Everyone would be on the lookout for stranded marine mammals. Whales were a bonus. They were huge and had lots of fat, which the herders would mix with ochre to rub on their bodies. If there were no whales, then seals would also provide oil. The mean size of seals at Kasteelberg was around 25 kilograms, just enough for a man to carry up to the site from the coast. At this age of death, young seals that died weighing 25 kg had achieved the optimal ratio of fat to meat weight. Experiments with marine-mammal fat have shown that it can be buried and will keep for about two weeks (Smith et al. 1992). This was recorded by early visitors to the Cape, including Johan Nieuhof in 1654, who described the Khoekhoen burying whale meat: 'From the whales and other sea monsters that are stranded they cut away the blubber and oily meat, and eat it with great relish … some cut pieces from these, and bury them under the sand, to eat later' (Raven-Hart 1971: 17).

Material culture

Like many African pastoralists, the Khoekhoen spent a great deal of time on their dress. This can be seen in Figures 6.2 and 6.4, as well as in the late-17th-century drawings in this chapter.

We are reliant on pictures like these to see what their dress really looked like. Archaeology does contribute to our understanding, but this evidence is mostly in the form of ostrich eggshell beads and some bones with holes pierced used in decoration. Other than dress and the pots they made, however, we know remarkably little about the rest of their material culture, except perhaps their huts, which are still in use in Namaqualand. As noted by Smith (2006: 10), Khoekhoe ethnographic material is extremely limited, not because objects might not have been collected, but because this mostly happened before formal collections were placed in museums. Most objects were part of private collections, many of which have been lost or dispersed over the years. The one collection that has survived is that of Swedish naturalist Anders Sparrman, made at the end of the 18th century and housed in the Museum of Ethnography in Stockholm (Rudner & Rudner 1957), but even this is limited: a basket, footwear, a horn smoking pipe, engraved ostrich eggs, a bow and arrows, two skin crowns decorated with cowries, a shell necklace and a rhino-bladder bottle.

As suggested before, we can assume, given the transient nature of their lifestyle, that almost everything they owned would be portable (except perhaps large grindstones), and this meant the use of skin bags to carry clothing, etc., and other containers of wood and skin (Figure 5.2). The exception, of course, would have been pottery, which could be used to carry liquids. Other than beads, or elephant ivory bracelets (Figure 6.1), which would have been for decoration, everything else had to be functional and made of organic material. Metals were rare. Native copper was known and came from Namaqualand. This was the reason for Cape governor Simon van der

109

Stel's trip north in 1685–1686 to find the source (Waterhouse 1932). Iron pieces came from the Xhosa to the east and were also used for decoration. So rare was iron that the first European arrivals could trade a cow for a knife, although later, when iron became more generally available, brass was preferred, as it could be made more easily into decorative objects. However, for the Khoekhoen wealth lay not in material goods but rather in their cattle.

Belief systems

It is not easy to know what religion the Khoekhoen had. Most observers appear either to have not been able to ask the right questions or to have been so disgusted at the lack of what they considered appropriate beliefs that they assumed the Khoekhoen had no religion. When an attempt was made to collect the information available, such as that of Grevenbroek (1933) in 1695, we are not sure that the concept of a Supreme Being or its opposite was not a result of Christian missionary activity. Even the idea of Khoe dancing at the full moon, which a number of people commented on, was not really properly investigated to determine if indeed this was a religious observance. Hahn (1881) gives the Supreme Being the name Tsuni-//Goam, to which the Khoekhoen give reverence.

Evans-Pritchard is very critical of attempts to define African religions. His work among the Nuer strongly points to the idea of 'Spirit'. To the Nuer, he says, '[t]he conception of ancestral ghosts is altogether subordinate. Animistic ideas are almost entirely absent. Witchcraft ideas play a very minor role

Figure 6.2: A Namaqua funeral: preparing the body (Gordon Archive, Rijksmuseum, Amsterdam).

and magic a negligible one ... there is no idea of an impersonal force ...' (Evans-Pritchard 1956: 316). He goes on to say that 'many representations of Spirit we find in Nuerland today are a fairly recent introduction and development ...' (Ibid: 317). This from an observer working with a pastoral group that was relatively isolated in the 1930s. We might be wary of trying to define religious beliefs among the Khoekhoen who,

111

Figure 6.3: Khoe chief's grave, covered with stones and bones (Gordon Archive, Rijksmuseum, Amsterdam).

by the end of the 19th century, when Hahn was writing, had mostly lost their traditional life and among whom missionary activity was strong.

That said, there might be an interface between Khoekhoen descendants and the spirit world that is still alive. Schmidt (2020) and Low (2014), working with local Nama and Damara in Namibia, discuss the 'new animism', which includes trickster and magical tales, as well as spirits that exist beside the road, manifest in large stone cairns. These need to be respected and added to, otherwise misfortune will happen.

The Khoekhoen chose to celebrate moments of transition, called !Nau, which were birth, changes to adulthood, marriage and death, all of which featured the slaughter of a sheep. The details of a young woman's first period and her seclusion while being mentored by an older woman are well documented by Hoernlé (1925). Colonel Robert Gordon did note in 1779–1780 that usually men did the slaughtering, but if a woman did so for a special occasion she had to wear a piece of mongoose skin on her head (Smith & Pheiffer 1992). The Kasteelberg site produced a fair number of mongoose bones, more than any other site excavated. Sometimes, when a large group was together, they would coat a lamb with ochre and sacrifice it to the good god who brought the beneficial rains, or to keep away the evil spirits. An example of such a small lamb skeleton was found at KBB. It was covered in ochre, while all the surrounding bones had none. This suggested a ritual sacrifice (Smith 2006).

Some observers said that the Khoe did not like to kill their cattle, although they would eat any animal that had died. Colonel Gordon, who made several long journeys into the interior in the 18th century, said that most ceremonies were accompanied by slaughter, often of a sheep, but wild buck were also included (Smith & Pheiffer 1992; Smith & Bull 2016).

Schapera (1930) has extensive notes on the burial practices of the Bushmen and Khoekhoen. These reflect beliefs about what causes death and how the dead are buried. In both cases, death is often ascribed to the actions of sorcerers or evil spirits, even when natural causes, such as age, are evident.

The burial practice of the Khoekhoen was observed by Colonel Gordon in 1779, and the depiction of the preparation of the body (Figure 6.2) is part of the Gordon Archive in Amsterdam. He also drew the grave of a wealthy Khoe, his status evident in the bones and head of an ox (Figure 6.3),

Figure 6.4: Flute band and dancing seen below the Kamiesberg, Namaqualand, in 1779 (Gordon Archive, Rijksmuseum, Amsterdam).

and showing the common practice of piling stones over the corpse to prevent scavenging by wild animals. A different style of burial was found during the Cobern Street excavations in Cape Town in 1994–1995. The body had been buried with knees to the chin in a sitting position (see Boonzaier et al. 1996: Figure 29). In 1818, Christian Latrobe also recorded an interesting feature when he attended a funeral at Genadendal. The body was interred in a niche, similar to Muslim burials at Prestwich Place in Cape Town. We do not know if there was any historical connection.

Among the Khoekhoen music had two subsets: sacred,

used to invoke the moon for help from a good spirit, perhaps to bring rain, and 'profane', or secular, where stories were told, or for dancing in !Nau celebrations. There is considerable detail on Khoisan music and dancing offered by Schapera (1930). Both have simple stringed instruments, such as a bow where the tone is altered by placing one end in the mouth. Khoekhoen flute bands made a very good impression on European visitors. Their flutes were made from reeds or, in drier areas, from the roots of acacia trees. Each flute played a different single note, so a 'band' of at least nine players produced a pleasant harmony for dancing. These flutes have disappeared but were heard first by Vasco da Gama in 1497 (Olivier 2006), and later by Colonel Gordon (in 1779) in Namaqualand (Figure 6.4), and by Alexander (1838) in southern Namibia.

Trade

It is not known when cannabis (dagga) was first introduced to the Khoekhoen. It seems to have existed by the time the earliest Dutch colonists set up at the Cape (Moodie 1838–1842: 225, although see Elphick 1985: 63 for discussion). It may have been offered in exchange by people further east. Similarly, as we have seen, metal was extremely rare. Iron might have come from the Xhosa in the east as well. The first iron among the Khoe was probably used as decoration, and iron was initially the main trade commodity with the first European visitors. Early commentators thought that this was because the Khoekhoen wanted to make weapons, but Sadr (2002) has noted that although there was a growth period in the 17th century before the colony was established, this dropped off after 1615, as the demand grew for brass instead. This suggests that the metals were more for decoration: brass is much more malleable than iron, at least within the limited capabilities of the Khoekhoen at that time. There were also increasing numbers of shipwrecks in Table Bay, so the herders could have had an additional resource from which to scavenge iron.

Exchange was probably quite restricted, as families were able to fend adequately for themselves without any outside needs. In many ways this was why the Khoekhoen misunderstood Dutch trading. The Khoekhoen had little idea about the extent of the maritime economic system of the VOC, even though a couple of them, such as Autshumao, had been interpreters and had even gone on ships to the Far East. This lack of understanding was why, during the two wars between the Khoe and the Dutch, the herders tried to steal the Dutch cattle, assuming this (as in Khoe society) to be the basis of their economy and authority at the Cape. The Khoe were quite effective at stealing cattle, especially when they learnt to time their raids during the rains, which made the colonists' muzzle-loading guns ineffective, but little could they conceive the expansive mercantile 'state' that the VOC controlled.

Equally, the Dutch settlers had no concept of the value of cattle to the Khoekhoen. These animals represented not just meat (as would have been assumed by the colonists), but were also integral to the Khoe social and economic way of life. This was the reason that Van Riebeeck complained about the Khoe being reluctant to exchange their animals when the Dutch first attempted to set up their base.

Inheritance

There is some confusion about how people inherited after the death of the family head. In 1721, Büttner said that all inheritance of the herd was through the male line, while the wife owned the hut and her belongings, although she could own some animals if they had been given to her before her husband died (Nienaber & Raven-Hart 1970: 91). Schapera (1930) basically agrees that male primogeniture prevailed among the Khoe, although he notes that there are some commentators who thought that Nama rules stated the wife should inherit, unless she returned to her family. In that case all the children would inherit equally. Since the rules were never written down, and all was organised orally, we can assume that the rest of the social group would have kept a close eye on who inherited what. What is important is that ownership was individual, unlike what would be deemed communal among hunters. This was particularly important with the animals held within the family.

Among the Khoe, day-to-day herd management around the kraal was primarily in the hands of women (Parsons & Lombard 2016) because they had to deal with milking and feeding the family. Men did spend a great deal of time hunting, but to assume that the cattle herds were not looked after, as Parsons and Lombard suggest, fails to recognise that there were always predators (both human and animal) around that had to be dealt with. Stealing cattle was one way a young man could obtain the animals he needed as bride-wealth to pay his prospective in-laws. Depending on the season, if the cattle had to be taken to pastures a long way from the household, then young people would stay with the animals. In this case, milch animals would be left at the kraal for women and children to use.

The Khoe Drawings

What the Khoekhoen actually looked like was bedevilled by the fact that virtually all early depictions were done in Europe by people who had never seen the Khoe personally, and who had to rely on crude descriptions, many of which emphasised their barbarity, by voyagers who had visited the Cape.

We are very fortunate that one traveller with artistic skills visited the Cape, probably en route to the Far East, at the end of the 17th century. The notebook he left behind has no author's name, so we can only surmise who he was from traveller's records and ship movements. We can, however, narrow down his period at the Cape from several sources. The watermarks on the paper he used can be dated between 1688 and 1707. There are several different scripts, the earliest of which was probably late 17th century.

The depictions of the Khoekhoen show them to be relaxed in dealing with Europeans. This would probably have been unlikely after the smallpox epidemic of 1713, which decimated the Khoekhoen, who had no immunity to the disease (Smith 1989). One name for the artist stands out as a possibility, that of Victor Victors, who was sent out to the colonies by Nicholas Witzen to gather information for his 'Atlas'. Victors' father, Jan Victors (1619–1679), was a student of Rembrandt in Holland, so there might have been

Figure 6.5: Khoe herder with his animals, late-17th-century drawing, National Library of South Africa (Smith & Pheiffer 1993: Plate 15).

the appropriate relationship and skills for the choice. Victors was probably chosen by Witzen along with Grevenbroek (1933), who spent some time at the Cape, and who was very sympathetic to Khoekhoe culture, having made great efforts to record their lifestyle by personal observation, and would also have contributed information about Witzen's collection.

The drawings were part of an artist's notebook separated into two sections for sale by Muller's in Amsterdam in 1882: 'Hottentots' at the Cape, and pictures of the Far East. The Cape section was bought by the librarian Fairbridge and given to the South African Library, where they were housed, but little attention was paid to them. Later, after they were found and catalogued by the iconographic section of the library, when it was set up in 1986, their history and context

119

Figure 6.6: Khoe women dancing, late-17th-century drawing, National Library of South Africa (Smith & Pheiffer 1993: Plate 13).

were examined and published (Smith & Pheiffer 1993; see also Smith 1995 for discussion).

The drawings give us details of how the Khoekhoen dressed. The skins of the animals they ate provided the clothes they wore. These consisted mostly of aprons hanging from the waist, but if it was cold a kaross could be draped around the shoulders (Figure 6.5). Women often wore caps decorated with beads, or had their hair neatly trimmed (Figures 6.6 and 6.7). They also wore ostrich-eggshell beads around their necks, and occasionally copper earrings. Rings of dried skin worn around their legs made a clicking sound when they walked or danced (Figure 6.6), and they also carried tasselled skin bags. Women

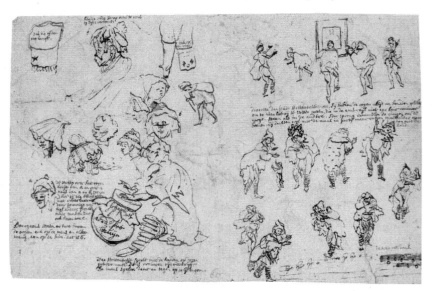

Figure 6.7: Page from the artist's notebook, late-17th-century drawing, National Library of South Africa (Smith & Pheiffer 1993: Plate 12).

enjoyed painting their faces with black lines across the nose (Figure 6.7). The men's clothes were similar, except the aprons tended to be shorter and were less likely to be decorated. They also wore ivory bracelets on their upper arms. These would be primarily decorative but could also deflect a blow from a spear while fighting. A man would often carry a fly whisk and a spear (Figure 6.1).

Figure 6.8 shows, on the left, an old woman with her broken stick and tattered clothes, with a colonial house in the background. On the right is a young woman, elegantly dressed in her fine clothes, with a traditional *matjieshuis* in the background. It is tempting to interpret these two images as

Figure 6.8: Two drawings of Khoe women, late 17th century, National Library of South Africa (Smith & Pheiffer 1993: Plate 9).

a statement by the artist of the negative effects of colonialism on the Khoekhoen and the deteriorating conditions of traditional life around the Dutch settlement at the Cape.

CHAPTER 7

Herders Meet Hunters

What effect might the arrival of herding people have had on the hunter-gatherers of southern Africa? For thousands of years hunters had known their land and had occupied all the ecological niches of the subcontinent, dispersed over seaside, mountains and deserts. When herders arrived with their domestic animals, how did this affect the local hunter-gatherers who had never seen the need to control animals in that way? Domestic animals are private property, with the possibility of some herders being more 'wealthy' than others. This would have been completely at odds with the idea of equal use of resources and sharing that is basic to southern African hunter-gatherer ideology, in which no individual owned anything other than personal hunting equipment (and even arrows were shared among the group). Areas of land and its resources might be considered occupied by specific groups, but the boundaries were flexible depending on conditions at any moment in time. Thus, if one group had a resource available to them, given good rainfall in their area, another contiguous group might approach and ask to use the better resources.

Permission would most likely be given, because reciprocity was expected, and as conditions changed, the situation could well reverse itself in the future, and a quid pro quo would have been expected. Equally, marriages occurred between groups, so sharing would have widened between in-laws.

Was the arrival of new groups an easy transition? There was probably little friction between groups, unless truly difficult conditions arose. However, there is evidence of interpersonal violence, found in skeletons along the west and south coasts of South Africa. In one study, perimortem trauma (injuries that most probably caused death) were restricted to around 2500 BP, and mostly involved women and children (Pfeiffer 2016). Another study of archaeological skulls (Gibbon & Davies 2020) showed that 39 per cent of them had perimortem trauma, and this was also higher in women. These skeletons were both pre- and post-2000 BP. In this sample, 19 per cent with ante-mortem trauma (injuries that healed) showed an increase after 2000 BP. What was notable in this study was that most of the trauma was not found on the facial region, but on the back and sides. This might fit with the unique 2 000-year-old skeletons from Faraoskop, in the Western Cape, where 12 individuals were excavated, several with head injuries that were probably fatal (Manhire 1993).

We have to ask ourselves: is it purely a coincidence that violence should occur at the same time that herders were arriving in southern Africa? Or was the period 2500–2000 BP, before the arrival of domestic animals, subject to contestation for different reasons, such as interference in marriage relations and pressures by new groups coming into the area, or for control over marine resources? Who might these new groups have been?

The arrival of herders in the Cape has produced different models of how this happened. Did hunters become herders, and were these the occupants of Kasteelberg? Sadr is convinced that as there were only minor changes from the pre-herding to the herding phases, this was 'compatible with the proposition that small-scale population movement (infiltration) may have played a role in bringing ceramics to the west coast' (Sadr 2018: 51). Unfortunately, this ignores the needs of husbandry in getting livestock to southern Africa. In their study of sheep herding in Asia, Dahl and Hjort (1976) make the point that for a herd of sheep to be sustainable, there must be a minimum of 60 animals. This was describing herders who were well adapted to their environment. Let us consider what it might be like to bring sheep all the way from East Africa to the Kalahari through the tsetse-free highlands of southern Tanzania and Zambia, to cross the Zambezi (a tsetse zone) with their stock, arriving just before 2000 BP. The herders then travelled to the Cape via the territories of two major linguistic groups (Ju and Tuu, seen in the substrates of Khoe language), a distance of over 2 500 kilometres within 100 years, passing through completely new lands and having to avoid potential poisonous plants (Smith 2014) on the way, while having to protect their stock against predators (certainly wild animals, and possibly strange people they encountered). A herd size of probably greater than 60 animals would probably have had to be necessary for successful migration. This would not have been a 'small-scale' enterprise. We must assume that the herders were not travelling with vast amounts of possessions. The archaeology can equally be read as their being able to adjust to local conditions (and to take local wives).

Hunter-fisher shellfish collectors

As briefly mentioned in Chapter 5, there is an anomaly at
the Cape: the existence of very large shell middens (known as
mega-middens), formed between 3000 and 2000 BP (Jerardino
et al. 2013). Similarly, enormous shell middens are also known
from the shores of Lake Victoria (Robertshaw et al. 1983),
called 'shell-mounds ... of the Wilton culture' by Leakey
(1936: 69). These East African middens have been associated
with Late Kansyore fisher-hunters of East Africa, who date to
around 3800 BP at Wadh Lang'o (Prendergast 2010) and 2900
BP at Siror (Dale & Ashley 2010). Is there a possible connection between these hunter-fishers of East Africa and southern
Africa? The rivers that parallel the tsetse-free corridor down
the highlands of Zambia (Brelsford 1946), Malawi and northern Mozambique (Da Costa 1967; Begg et al. 2005) to the
Zambezi and on to the northern Kalahari (Dornan 1925;
Cashdan 1986) have fishers who build weirs and traps very
similar to what has been recorded around Lake Victoria (see
also Maclaren 1958).

The hunter-fishers along the Boteti and Nata rivers of the
northern Kalahari are eastern Khoe Bushmen, among whom
are Shua and Tshwa (Barnard 1992). Could they be similar to
the mythical Batwa who inhabited the rivers to the north in
Zambia and Malawi before the arrival of Iron Age farmers
(see Smith and Begg 2017)? These people were described by
Leyland (1866: 171–172):

> The principal tribe located on the Zouga (Botete) River
> is the Bakoba or slaves ... much darker and more

muscular than the Bechuana Kaffirs. They subsist principally upon fish, caught in large numbers with nets and spears ... Their views are in some respects totally opposite to the Bechuana of the south; the latter have a superstition attached to fish, believing that the rivers ... will dry up, if fish are caught and taken out ... The language of the Bakoba is similar to that of the Bushmen, with a click.

Fishing traps and baskets made from woven reeds were used even further south along the Fish River in southern Namibia (Alexander 1838, vol 1: 237) and along the Orange River (Schapera 1930: 138). In 1887, a note in the *Orange Free State Monthly Magazine* compared the Caledon River around Bethulie, near its juncture with the Orange/Gariep, to what Sir Samuel Baker had seen at the northern end of Albert Nyanza (Lake Albert) on the Uganda side (Skotnes 1996: 200). Stow also observed that fishing nets and baskets used on Albert Nyanza and the Orange River were the same, which he attributed to a southern migration (Stow 1905: 93).

As we will see in Chapter 8, there is an apparent lack of genetic evidence for any pre-Iron Age herders in southwestern Angola (Oliveira et al. 2017; 2018), but there is a possible connection between people living today on one of the northerly tributaries of the Kunene River and the Shua riverine-adapted people of northern Botswana. Again, rivers are the common denominator.

The Kansyore could have been a good source for the domestic animals and pottery that were introduced to southern

Africa, but if there was indeed a connection to the shellfish collectors, this may have predated the arrival of domestic animals. Such a scenario might suggest an earlier immigration by hunter-fishers looking for new lands and resources for trade, as hinted at by Alexander (1984). These hunters could have sent information back to East Africa about the good pasture lands to the south (Smith 2016) and encouraged the movement of domestic sheep out of East Africa.

A study of fishermen and fishing camps along the Lugenda Valley in Niassa National Park, northern Mozambique (Begg et al. 2005), showed that although 76 per cent of the people in the fishing camps were from nearby villages, outsiders did come in during the fishing season after the rains had stopped. Only then could the rock gabions that hold the fishing nets be rebuilt. These rock structures would have been similar across all the fishing groups, and require considerable effort to construct. Although this is a modern study, it does indicate how fishing culture is not static, and how people can move between different fishing zones.

It has already been noted in Chapter 5 that there seems to be a genetic connection between East and southern Africa seen in the Y-chromosome (A1b1b2) similarity in the St Helena Bay and Faraoskop skeletons (both dated to before 2000 BP) and pastoral skeletons from Kenya (see Table 8.1). A forensic study of the St Helena Bay skeleton showed it had 'surfer's ear', a condition resulting from immersion in the cold water of the Atlantic over a good period of the individual's life. Subsequent study has shown that two more skulls in the UCT collection also have the same condition. Schapera (1930: 304) notes of the Khoekhoen: 'They had no boats, but they were fearless swimmers and boldly threw themselves into the sea to reach a neighbouring rock, from which they fished with hook and line or harpooned the fish with their long wooden spears attached to a line.'

But the question still remains: who might have been the original donors of domestic stock from East Africa, and why was there a pastoral movement southward? There are several potential donors of the livestock: a) Kansyore from southern Kenya and northern Tanzania (Prendergast 2010); b) Savanna Pastoral Neolithic (SPN) found in southern Kenya (Ambrose 1984); and c) Elmenteitan from southern Kenya and northern Tanzania (Robertshaw 1990). All of these exhibit different cultural attributes and ratios of wild to domestic taxa on sites (Mutundu 2010). SPN and Elmenteitan are generally regarded as pastoral societies, while Kansyore have been seen primarily as fisher-foragers.

The reasons for the expansion of stock (and stock keepers) out of East Africa may have been the arrival of Iron Age farmers (Urewe) from West Africa in the region around 2500 BP, along the northern edge of the tropical forest, putting pressure on land and resources. Another reason, perhaps building on this emigration, could also have been delayed-return fisher-foragers taking up herding (Prendergast 2010) and moving south to avoid competition with established pastoralists. The similarities of pottery of early herders between East and southern Africa are not strong, although the Elmenteitan pottery from Ngamuriak (Robertshaw 1990) has been seen as possibly having some attributes in common with the early types at the Cape, particularly the use of spouts (Smith 2005).

129

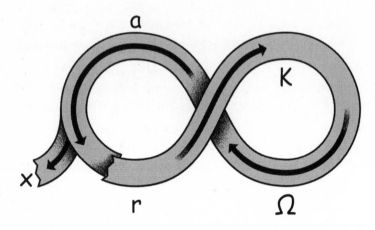

Figure 7.1: Resilience and transformation model (after Redman & Kinzig 2003).

Resilience theory

Looking at the genetic and linguistic data, we might offer a way to understand the steps herders took in adjusting to new environments and people by using resilience theory, or 'panarchy' (Gunderson & Holling 2002), a feedback mechanism whereby ecological and social systems can be modelled as going through various vicissitudes, such as migration, and rebounding. Resilience theory is used as an explanatory principle for adaptation in societies going through change, possibly under stress from outside forces. It can provide the means to understand long-term shifts leading to the adaptation, or demise, of cultures. It assumes that any society is basically flexible, and that members are capable of adjusting to pressure, but that people, unlike natural systems, have the additional stress of political vagaries that are more difficult to generalise about.

There are four stages recognised by resilience theorists, who use the concept to describe social systems (Figure 7.1):

1   Release or Ω phase: when internal fragility occurs due to pressure from external or internal agents.
2   Reorganisation or α phase: where resources (and social structures) can opportunistically be adjusted to form a new system.
3   Growth or r phase: rapid colonisation to take advantage of disrupted areas (or political conditions), but if the society does not reach this stage, the opportunity may be lost.
4   Conservation or K phase: energy (or ideas, such as technology) is slowly accumulated to allow maturity (Redman & Kinzig 2003).

Redman and Kinzig (2003: 5) go on to say: 'Adaptive capacity is enhanced by a rich social memory of alternative situations and responses, and by the accumulation of social capital in the form of the networks of trust, shared knowledge, and actual materials needed to facilitate (adaptive) responses.' This adaptive cycle is particularly useful in describing how small-scale societies are capable of surviving, as these often 'act conservatively, with strong traditions that are slow to change' (Redman & Kinzig 2003: 9). These could have included hunters of East and southern Africa, who probably conformed to this model of a relatively closed network maintained by the resilience-feedback system over considerable periods of time. Long-term separation

131

of the groups is indicated, for example, by the mutually unintelligible languages of Ju and Tuu. Once food producers arrived on the scene, these systems came under threat, and both hunter-gatherers and herders/farmers had to adjust accordingly.

The basic opportunism of foraging societies allows a degree of linguistic flexibility and accommodation (sometimes with language loss). Did this also mean economic adaptation? It is possible, but modern Kalahari hunters generally seem to maintain a focus on hunting even when small-stock herds exist. Their subsistence gathering is a generalist strategy, and goat herds are seen 'as merely additional elements which are added to the subsistence mix and thus serve to broaden even further the resource base' (Yellen 1984: 57). This underlines their flexibility, but the herds are allowed to take care of themselves, even when predators are in the vicinity, indicating that animal husbandry continues to play a lesser role compared with hunting activities.

Table 7.1: Resilience theory and the COVID-19 trajectory

Phase	Characteristics
Ω	Virus arrives
α	Lockdown: schools closed, work stopped, travel halted
r	Deaths spike, then drop Phased reopening
K	Vaccinations: 'new normal'

To illustrate how the resilience-feedback model works, here is an example that the entire world has recently been faced with: the COVID-19 pandemic (Table 7.1).

The r phase is the crucial one. This is when the participants/agents must build on the reorganisation sufficiently so that they can move on to the final K phase. This means using what is on offer (or can be found), and trying to use the alternatives to rework what existed before, that is, to 'fill in the cracks' that have been identified (for example, in the modern context, the Black Lives Matter movement).

Modelling the expansion of domestic stock from East Africa

Looking for the original expansion of domestic stock into southern Africa requires some idea of the conditions elsewhere in Africa from where they might have come. The animals had to come from the north, as no wild progenitors of the domestic animals of southern Africa (sheep, goats, cattle, donkeys) exist in the subcontinent. There is every reason to believe that the animals were introduced overland, although the intervening area between East and southern Africa has no data to offer yet, except for the possibility of undated rock paintings from Zimbabwe depicting fat-tailed sheep. A sea connection can probably be ruled out, even though Indian Ocean trade with East Africa is over 2000 years old (Mitchell 2002), since travelling by sea south of the equator was difficult before the invention of the moveable lateen sail used on Arab dhows. Not only were epizootic diseases (transmitted between different species) a problem that could inhibit expansion of the animals, in particular the distribution of tsetse flies, which carry nagana, or sleeping

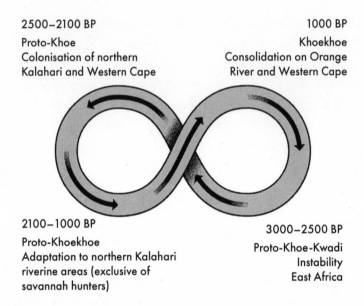

2500–2100 BP

Proto-Khoe
Colonisation of northern
Kalahari and Western Cape

1000 BP

Khoekhoe
Consolidation on Orange
River and Western Cape

2100–1000 BP

Proto-Khoekhoe
Adaptation to northern Kalahari
riverine areas (exclusive of
savannah hunters)

3000–2500 BP

Proto-Khoe-Kwadi
Instability
East Africa

Figure 7.2: Resilience adaptation of herders moving from East to southern Africa, and the development of Khoekhoe language (Andrew Smith).

sickness, but connection via the tropical forest area of West Central Africa can be ruled out, as this is not an environment conducive to herding.

Resilience theory can be used to model how herders responded to complexity in East Africa when farmers entered the area between 3000 and 2500 BP (Phase Ω). Figure 7.2 is the simplest model showing how colonisation (Phase α) via the tsetse-free corridor provided a bolthole to relieve the pressures on land and resources. This may have caused a 'bow wave' (Alexander 1984) of herders moving southwards with their stock, reaching the Kalahari before 2000 BP and developing the Khoe-Kwadi language. Güldemann (2008: 118) argues that the first domestic stock arrived with people who 'spoke an early chronolect of the Khoe-Kwadi family [and] had a Non-Khoisan genetic profile'. This might be supported by the Y-chromosome identified by Henn et al. (2008) as being Nilotic (from East Africa), or the A1b1b2 signature seen in both East Africa and the Western Cape of South Africa (see Table 8.1).

Those herders who stayed in the northern Kalahari (Phase r) adapted to the riverine systems of the Botletle (northern Botswana) and Nata (southwestern Zimbabwe), setting up delayed-return fishing communities, and excluding savannah hunters from river frontage, as is seen today (Cashdan 1986), while adopting some of the language from the Ju-speakers (Proto-Khoe).

While conditions may initially have been good for pastoralism before 2000 BP, they probably deteriorated soon thereafter. This meant some important decisions had to be made. Some herders stayed in the northern Kalahari, but others opted to try their luck further south towards another river system, the Vaal/Orange. Tuu-speakers living here introduced a substrate into the proto-Khoekhoe language. This movement allowed consolidation of the herds and rapprochement with local hunter-gatherers, especially when the herders expanded into the Cape 2 000 years ago, where the Khoekhoe language developed (Phase K).

As noted above, the r phase is crucial. The herders arriving in the Western Cape had access to new and better pastures and water. They had local hunter-gatherers to teach them about what was on offer (seasonal/different foods, marine resources, medicines, wives, etc). Were they just blundering through and being opportunistic, or did they value what was on offer, and build upon it? If the Kasteelberg 'B' site is any indication, they made good choices, because their economic base grew well.

The herders may also have gone towards KwaZulu-Natal, where non-Iron Age pottery from the first millennium AD has been found (Mazel 1992), and into highland Lesotho. Two sites in highland Lesotho, Likoaeng and Sehonghong, dated to the first millennium AD, produced potsherds with milk residues adhering (Fewlass et al. 2020). These thin-walled ceramics from sites ostensibly occupied by hunter-gatherers (Mitchell 1996) are not Iron Age, and are even called 'hunter-gatherer' pottery. We might challenge this identification, since thin-walled pottery is what was found on herder sites further north, for example at Geduld in Namibia (Smith & Jacobson 1995) and all the way across to Limpopo province (Hall & Smith 2000) and the Waterberg (Mari van der Ryst, personal communication) (see Figure 5.1) and in pre-Iron Age sites in KwaZulu-Natal (Mazel 1992). Thus, we have the possibility of close cooperation between hunter-gatherers and incoming herders, at least until Early Iron Age farmers occupied the area, when the existence of Proto-Khoe-speakers (Güldemann 2008) could have been subsumed into more powerful polities. Unfortunately, no sheep bones have been found on the KwaZulu-Natal sites (Mazel 1992). An interesting idea offered by Ehret (1982) is that the 'Limpopo-Khoikhoi' are only known from loan words in Bantu languages, such as the words for 'cow' and '(sour) milk'. Souring leads to changes in the milk that allow consumption by people who are lactose-intolerant, such as the hunter-gatherers of southern Africa.

As we can see in Figure 7.1, the r phase is crucial in deciding the direction any society makes in the resilience cycle. The

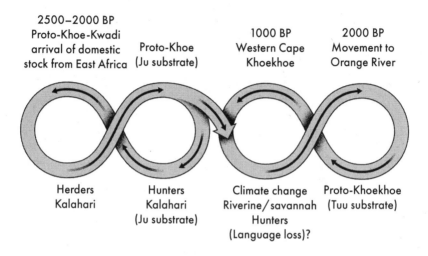

2500–2000 BP
Proto-Khoe-Kwadi
arrival of domestic   Proto-Khoe
stock from East Africa   (Ju substrate)

1000 BP
Western Cape
Khoekhoe

2000 BP
Movement to
Orange River

Herders   Hunters   Climate change   Proto-Khoekhoe
Kalahari   Kalahari   Riverine/savannah   (Tuu substrate)
                (Ju substrate) Hunters
                               (Language loss)?

Figure 7.3: Resilience adaptation of herders to climatic change in the northern Kalahari (Andrew Smith).

group may not be able to adapt, so might disappear or go in a different direction. Using this idea, we might be able to model the difference between what happened to the Khoekhoen who ultimately established themselves along the western and southern coasts (Figure 7.2) and those herders who went southeast to colonise the Lesotho and KwaZulu-Natal Drakensberg. These latter herders would have been close to the r phase of their cycle. The fact that they were not able to proceed to their K phase was due to their encapsulation by the arrival of Early Iron Age farmers around 300 AD, whose K phase would have been accomplished by the Later Iron Age, at the end of the first millennium AD.

Figure 7.3 shows the impact of the arrival of herding, accepting the climate change in the Kalahari after 2400 BP

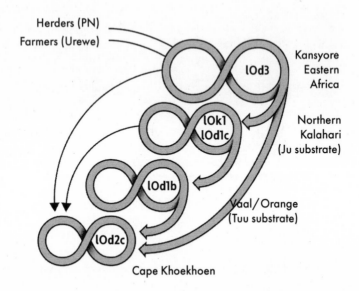

Figure 7.4: Transformation and resilience modelling of mtDNA haplogroups across East and southern Africa (Andrew Smith).

as an important catalyst for the spread of domestic animals, and for the development of the Khoekhoen. This model shows transformation of the social environment, as both hunter-gatherers and herders would have had to adjust to less favourable rainfall conditions, either by solidifying the controls over riverine zones of the Kalahari or by moving south to colonise new river systems.

Resilience-theory modelling provides a means to demonstrate how hunting groups maintain a degree of equilibrium even in adversity induced by environmental change. However, the introduction of new economic systems may have required

138

transformation to a new state by some groups, either as herders themselves or as lower-status groups within the social hierarchy. Alternatively, although southern African hunter-gatherers had to accommodate the new arrivals at one level, indicated by the degree of linguistic overlap, and by the possible loss of access to riverine resources, the appearance of domestic animals on the landscape may only have widened the resource base of other groups.

Using a resilience-theory model (Figure 7.4), we might suggest that each stage of the southward journey would have required adjustments on the part of the herders and their animals to new physical environments with different plants (some of which might have been poisonous enough to make the animals sick, if not prove fatal) (Smith 2014), and to new people who spoke different languages, had different customs and might be able to assist the newcomers in adjusting to an unusual environment. Such an adjustment might include the use of medicinal and other useful plants (see Appendix). Each phase of the herders' migration meant contact with new genetic groups, and admixtures, also seen in the substrates of Khoe languages.

A more nuanced view?

There is a tendency to think that the incoming herders were the dominant force in the new relationship between Khoe and the Tuu hunter-gatherers of South Africa, since that seems to have been the case when the first European observers arrived. In his detailed linguistic analysis, Güldemann (2006: 128) looks at this differently: 'Hunter-gatherers can have a profound influence on the language of newcomers.' He sees the influence of the Tuu language on Khoe as being more than cursory, so the idea of a 'substrate' (Figure 8.1) in Khoe-khoe should be seen as more than just casual. If this is true, then it puts their relationship on a very different footing: the hunter-gatherers would initially have been a more important part of the herder adjustment to the new social and physical environment. This may have resulted in a much more equal relationship to start with than would ultimately develop once cattle ownership became the mainstay of Khoekhoe social life in the second millennium AD.

An interesting perspective is offered by Wittenberg (2012), who looks at the folk tales of both the Khoekhoen and Bushmen. While acknowledging the limited voice of both hunter-gatherers and herders to have come down to us in the 21st century, these tales still resonate within rural communities (De Prada-Samper 2016). In Wittenberg's analysis, jackals are important players in the stories of Khoekhoen, where they are tricksters who 'outfox' lions. In the later narratives this can be seen as a form of satire where the lions are replaced by farmers (boers). This could happen in a hierarchical society where herders can own private stock and can be seen as a form of resistance against colonial rule.

In contrast, the Bushman stories have the praying mantis (/Kaggen) as their trickster, whose role supports the inherent sharing ethos of hunters. Wittenberg gives an example of when there might be crossing-over of stories: the son of a Korana chief and a /Xam (Bushman) mother narrates a jackal tale in which, although the lion is defeated, the emphasis in the outcome is on the need to share meat among the group.

Wittenberg also suggests that the /Xam stories about the jackal that were given to Bleek and Lloyd (1911) were mediated through Khoekhoe intermediaries.

Another clue to the impact of Bushman life on the Khoekhoen might be in the structure of huts. As the incoming herders were probably almost as mobile as the indigenous hunters, not only herding their sheep but also being active hunters themselves, the herders might have learnt the simple way of building a hut from the hunter-gatherers. This allows for much greater mobility than the homestead-with-garden model common among pastoralists further north. The hunter's technique is to fashion a simple framework of saplings in a ring, which, when tied together at the top, forms a dome. This would be finished off by coating the outside with leafy vegetation (thick when there were rains, thin when only shade was needed). The use of mats to cover the framework could have come later among the herders, especially when they had the odd ox available to transport the rolled-up covering.

The use of hut space is very similar among both modern hunter-gatherers (Figure 7.5) and the extant herders of the Richtersveld in the Northern Cape (Figure 7.6), who still use the *matjieshuis* (Haacke 1982). Where the idea of woven, flexible plant material came from is not clear. It certainly exists among farming communities, but is not used by other herders of southern Africa, such as the Himba, who tend to use more durable (and immovable) structures of wattle and daub as fixed reference points to where they can return. Woven fibres, however, are an important fixture of fisher-herder societies who have need of nets and baskets. A variation on the theme, not recorded in the more recent time period, is the use

141

Figure 7.5: Hut used by Ju/'hoansi hunters in northern
Namibia, a simple structure using branches (Andrew Smith).

of skin covering, either instead of mats or over mats, by the
Groot Namaquas. An example of this was illustrated by the
18th-century French naturalist François Le Vaillant (Quinton
& Lewin Robinson 1973, Vol I: Plate 56).

Among the Nama, a woman owns her hut. The husband
might help erect the structure, but the wife makes the mats that
clad the hut. Brink (2004) stresses the importance of cultural
identity imbued in Khoe huts and settlement areas, even if
they were transhumant. A woman's identity with the domestic
structure is in the ash heap on the outside, where the fire remains
are deposited each morning. No other woman would usurp
this space (Smith & Webley 2000). It can be seen in Figure
7.6 that the hut structure is left in place today, possibly to
be used at some later date. There is a very fine drawing by

142

Figure 7.6: Abandoned campsite in the Richtersveld, showing the dome structure with the mats removed, and the outside *werf* (yard) where cooking and socialising would be done (Andrew Smith).

Samuel Daniel, done in 1805, of a Khoekhoe encampment being prepared for movement. The ox is shown carrying some of the structural poles.

While these are modern ethnographic examples, at the very bottom of the excavations at Kasteelberg, dated to the first millennium AD, holes were found that suggest the base of hut structures dug into the ground (Mutti 2006). If these were indeed postholes and the base for huts, then this demonstrates that there was considerable time-depth to the type of structure described for the herders during the colonial period. This type of structure would then predate the emergence of the Khoekhoen.

Of course, these huts could describe a generic mobile camp

structure, as seen by Gulliver (1951: 73) among the Turkana herders of northern Kenya: 'The night hut is a dome skeleton structure about four feet high in the middle, and about six or seven feet in diameter. It is made of rounded lengths of wood interwoven and tied together, with a small gap left for the entrance. At nights to afford shelter against winds and cool air, and when it is raining, cattle hides are spread over the outside of this frame and tied down with leather thongs.'

All this neatly coincides with the aDNA reading of the Kasteelberg girl (see Chapter 5), who has a strong southern Bushman signature, as well as genetic contact with East African pastoralists. The latter would not have casually taken southern Bushman wives but would have become strongly embedded in their society, so that by the time of the early colonists at the Cape, the phenotype (physical appearance) of both the Bushmen and the Khoekhoen was virtually indistinguishable, although their languages and culture still remained separate. This is suggested in a report of 6 December 1660 in which Jan Dankaert says of the Soaqua: 'They are rather modest, but in their speech they also cluck like turkey-cocks, the more so as one goes further into the interior. Among the Hottentot race there is also one language which all their great ones understand but which the common people do not' (Thom 1958: 300).

CHAPTER 8

Configuring Khoisan Linguistics and Genomics

Research into Bushman prehistory and Khoekhoe origins has been vastly augmented by recent linguistic and genetic studies. These have complemented each other, as awareness of the important part southern African First Nations people have played in modern human development has grown.

Linguistic variation: Kx'a (Ju), Tuu and Khoe

In southern Africa, as far as the Bushman languages spoken today are concerned, there exist two main groupings: Kx'a (mostly Ju, spoken in the Kalahari of northern Namibia and Botswana) and Tuu (spoken in southern Namibia and Botswana, and formerly in the interior of South Africa, but now mostly extinct there). Linguistically speaking, although they are both click-speaking, these two hunting populations are mutually exclusive. They cannot speak to each other unless they learn each other's language (Petersen et al. 2013).

The third 'click' language in southern Africa is the

separate Khoe family, which may have an East African origin, since Sandawe hunters of Kenya and Khoe have mutual derivatives. This developed as Khoe-Kwadi language in the northern Kalahari (Güldemann 2008).

Older linguistic studies rely on word comparisons to relate languages to each other. While this might work with languages that are very close, such as French and English, modern linguistic studies focus on how languages are structured. There are a number of differences between Khoe and the Bushman languages. For example, in Khoe the verb position in a clause is at the end, while in the Bushman languages it is in the middle of the clause. Khoe has no prepositions, while the Bushman languages do have prepositions (Güldemann 2008: Table 2).

Güldemann's model of Khoe language (Figure 8.1) shows distinct separation between the Kalahari branch and the Khoekhoe. According to Güldemann, the different Khoekhoe groups virtually all speak the same language, so have not been separated for long enough to develop distinctive differences, certainly less than 2 000 years.

The rapid spread of domestic stock has to take cognisance of linguistic evidence of Bushman language 'substrates' in Khoekhoe language (Güldemann 2008). As can be seen in Figure 8.1, only the Ju substrate can be found in the northern Proto-Khoe dialects, while both Ju and Tuu substrates exist in Khoekhoe dialects. This would indicate that these languages may have converged with the passing of migrants through the areas where they were spoken.

Was there enough time for the immigrant herders to absorb linguistic elements from the local languages spoken in the lands they passed through, or did the first immigrants not yet

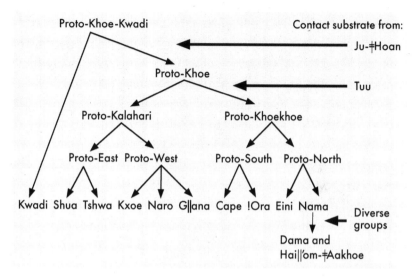

Figure 8.1: Development of Khoe languages (from Güldemann 2008: Figure 2; used with permission).

speak Khoekhoe, and this developed later? When the Dutch first set up their refreshment station at the Cape in the mid-17th century, they met coastal foragers called Soaqua (Sonqua) by the Khoekhoen. The two references to the languages of 'these small people' (as they were distinguished by Dutch observers) are clues to their speaking a different tongue to the Khoekhoen.

On 3 April 1655, Jan Wintervogel stated that they met Soaqua, who were 'people of very small stature, subsisting very meagrely, quite wild, without huts, cattle or anything in the world, clad in small skins like these Hottentots and speaking almost as they do' (Thom 1952: 305), possibly meaning they both had clicks in their speech.

The observation that the Khoekhoen had hunters as clients

to do menial tasks was noted by Simon van der Stel during his trip to Namaqualand (16 September 1685): '[W]e find that these Sonquas are just the same as the poor in Europe, each tribe of Hottentots having some of them and employing them to bring news of the approach of a strange tribe. They steal nothing from the kraals of their employers, but regularly from other kraals ... possessing nothing ... except what they acquire by theft' (Waterhouse 1932: 122). Kolb (1731, Vol 1: 76) stated that the 'Sonquas are mercenaries to other Hottentot nations, serving for food.'

Unfortunately, unlike the Khoekhoe language spoken at the Cape when the first Europeans settled, there are no surviving records of anyone having written any detailed information about the Sonqua language. Thus, we have no way of knowing if it was indeed a different language to that of the Khoekhoen, and, if so, how it may have related to other Bushman languages spoken in South Africa, such as /Xam, a Tuu language of the interior (Bleek & Lloyd 1911). In fact, how far south the /Xam language may have spread towards the coast is also unknown.

The fact that the extant Kx'a and Tuu languages are mutually unintelligible today would suggest a long period of separation between the speakers of these languages. This could be seen not only as a linguistic separation but also as the genetic isolation of groups with limited impact from the outside, or little movement between groups (see Table 8.2). The separation between Kx'a and Tuu languages has a genetic component. The haplogroup LOk1 occurs north of the Orange/Gariep River, and so among the Kx'a speakers, and is not found among the southern San descendants, such as the

Karretjiemense of the Karoo (the *karretjie* is a donkey cart). We also have to consider the environmental changes due to climatic shifts that happened during the early Holocene, which could have affected the distribution of different human groups. Environmental shifts most probably put pressure on the fauna of southern Africa. By 9 500 years ago, four very large animals became extinct: giant buffalo, giant hartebeest, Cape horse and southern springbok. This is unlikely to have been solely due to hunting pressures (Mitchell 2002).

Such conservatism is perhaps what we might expect from hunting/foraging groups with good resources and relatively restricted territories, and which might be expressed in the theoretical feedback modelling of resilience theory described in Chapter 7.

Genomics of modern Khoisan groups

The basic genetic principle of greatest variability among populations gives them the greater time depth. In the case of the Bushmen, we are now aware that they are the most diverse of any living human population. Whether this means all humans are derived from ancestral Bushmen, as claimed by Chan et al. (2019), is still an open question because these are isolated populations, and we do not yet know what languages and genes may have disappeared further north in the continent. This is due to Africa-wide genomics lagging behind other parts of the world.

Although we are all made up of simple cellular structures, the way they are strung together as a double helix combining base pairs A/T and C/G, which make up the 46 chromosomes in each human cell, are the result of our ancestral history. We get our genes from each parent (mtDNA from the maternal line, and Y-chromosomes from the paternal line), and these can be identified, giving each of us our special lineage. While a blood sample from a living person can offer the complete genome, in skeletons that have been buried for many years the genetic strands might be broken and only small sections survive. Using modern technology, however, the specialist can still use these broken strands to recreate the ancient genomic signature. As mentioned above, the most complex genetic history in the world today is to be found among the Bushmen of southern Africa, indicating that they are the oldest surviving lineages.

In southern Africa the aboriginal maternal genes (mtDNA) are defined by the haplogroups LOd and LOk, which probably existed some 100 000 years ago. As noted above, LOk appears not to have existed south of the Orange/Gariep River, so is excluded from Tuu-speakers and their descendants in South Africa, such as the Karretjiemense: 'From the groups that represent the people with southern Khoe-San ancestry, the Karretjie People and ≠Khomani groups had almost exclusive LOd maternal lines' (Schlebusch et al. 2013: 16).

LOd3 is a very old lineage that has been found in low frequencies in both Tanzania and southern Africa. It has been separated into an East African subgroup, LOd3a, with a suggested diversion time of ±41 000 years from the southern African haplotypes (Schlebusch et al. 2013). This gives some idea of a maternal connection that may have existed between the two areas in the distant past. Two hunter groups in East

Africa, Hadza and Sandawe, share Khoisan ancestry with ≠Khomani and Ju/'hoansi hunters, as well as with descendants of southern hunters, such as the Karretjiemense (Shriner et al. 2018). This separation is calculated as being at least 30 000 years (Tishkoff et al. 2007).

This hypothesis, that admixture existed between Khoisan groups in East and southern Africa, is supported by work of Pickrell et al. (2012) and Schlebusch et al. (2020). Genetic information also shows a more recent specific Y-chromosome (male) connection between East and southern Africa (Henn et al. 2008; Barbieri et al. 2014).

The East African connection is further strengthened by the large corpus of 41 skeletons, most of which are identified as 'Pastoral Neolithic', sequenced in Prendergast et al. (2019), which shows Y-chromosome signatures that also appear in southern Africa. As can be seen in Table 8.1, the A1b1b2 signature from the Naivasha Burial Site and Keringet Cave in Kenya has also been found in two skeletons from the Western Cape: St Helena Bay and Faraoskop. The dates for these skeletons are within the period 2500–2000 BP. Does this mean a pre-herder connection between East Africa and the Western Cape? Or is it tied into the earliest arrival of food producers? From these 41 East African skeletons we also have to note that there were no L0d mtDNA signatures. In the available data, L0d is mostly restricted to southern Africa, although we see it in one of the Fingira skeletons, which showed L0d1b2b dated to 5270 BP (Table 8.1), much older than the others, and there are possible traces in Sandawe, a click-speaking hunter group of East Africa (Tishkoff et al. 2007).

Table 8:1: Potential aDNA links between East and southern Africa

Location	NRY-chromosome	mtDNA
St Helena Bay (2330 ±25 BP), Western Cape	A1b1b2a	LOd2c1
Kasteelberg 'B' (1310 ±50 BP), Western Cape		LOd1a1a
Faraoskop (2000 ±50 BP), Western Cape	A1b1b2a	LOd1b2b1b
Fingira (5270 ±25 BP), Malawi		LOd1b2b
Fingira (5290 ±25 BP), Malawi		LOd1c
Luxmanda (2925 ±20 BP), Tanzania		L2a1
Naivasha Burial Site (2255 ±20 BP), Kenya	A1b1b2b	
Keringet Cave (2465 ±20 BP), Kenya	A1b1b2	

Source: Skoglund et al. 2017; Prendergast et al. 2019.

The pastoral connection is further supported by Coelho et al. (2009: 15), who are of the opinion 'that the East African lactase persistence -14010C mutation [which allows humans to metabolise raw milk] has been carried to southern Africa by Khoe herders who contacted East African pastoralists'. This

Figure 8.2: Technique of encouraging a cow to release its milk, late-17th-century drawing, National Library of South Africa (Smith & Pheiffer 1993: Plate 16).

gene was also found in some hunter groups, supporting the idea of genetic mixture between hunters and herders (Breton et al. 2014; Macholdt et al. 2014).

The Khoekhoen were descended from this line of African herders. We see within Khoe society a number of traits found further north, such as the riding of oxen, depicted in Saharan rock art. There is also a milking technique seen in this art that is found within pastoral societies all the way south from the Sahara (Fauvelle-Aymar 2008; Le Quellec 2011). This includes herding societies in the West African Sahel, Sudan and Kenya, and among the Khoekhoen. The technique is called 'air insufflation' whereby the herder encourages milk flow from a recalcitrant animal, which may have lost its calf, by blowing into its rear end (Figure 8.2) (Fauvelle-Aymar 2008).

Barbieri et al. (2014: 444) also note, however, that 'admixture with immigrants did not leave evident traces in the maternal genetic material'. This strongly hints at the idea that males coming into southern Africa, probably bringing livestock with them, some 2 000 years ago, had few of their women with them, and so took wives from local hunter populations. In support of what has been mentioned earlier, Morris et al. (2014) note that the lineages LOk1a and LOd1c, found among hunter-gatherers of the Kalahari, are absent south of the Orange/Gariep River. They further argue that unlike food producers, such as Iron Age farmers or Khoe pastoralists, there was much greater stability among hunter-gatherer haplogroups.

An attempt to identify early food producers in southern Angola (Oliveira et al. 2017; 2018) failed to show any impact before the arrival of Himba/Herero Bantu-speaking pastoralists, who are thought to be Later Iron Age intrusions (Mitchell 2002: Figure 12.1). When the Himba/Herero first arrived in southern Angola is not known, although they were certainly there when the first Portuguese emissaries arrived in the 16th century. This may reflect minimal intrusion on the part of early herders, even though an Early Iron Age connection has been made between northern Angola and northern Botswana from Benfica (Denbow 1990) (see Figure 5.6). If the Himba/Herero arrival was indeed Later Iron Age and their cattle herds the result of equatorial farmers meeting pastoralists in East Africa, we might have an analogy with what happened in the Near East, where specialised pastoralism developed early out of agricultural society as herders focused more and more on their livestock, and there was space to expand into. However, Oliveira et al. (2017) make an interesting genetic connection (LOd1a1b1a) between living people of southwestern Angola and the Shua of northern Botswana. Would this be part of the first arrival of hunter-fishers into southern Africa that was suggested in Chapter 7?

LOd2c is the mtDNA of the first ancient genome to be sequenced from a West Coast skeleton, dated to 2300 BP (Morris et al. 2014) (see Table 8.1). The significance of this is to show that the coastal genetic signature is different from that of the interior. In addition, only the Nama samples from north of the Orange/Gariep River have a similar high frequency of LOd2c, but with a long genetic separation from the Cape West Coast individual. This implies that the Khoekhoe-speaking Nama herders came into contact with coastal foragers, such as those seen by Colonel Gordon at the mouth of the Orange River on 20 August 1779 (Raper & Boucher 1988: 270) (Figure 2.4), and also that the mtDNA signature of LOd2c may have been widespread up the West Coast, even though the populations at the Cape and those north of the Orange River may not have been in contact for a very long time.

Schlebusch (2010) has noted that there were two population expansion periods for LOd1: 14 000 and 3 000 years ago. The Fingira skeleton, dated to 5 300 years ago, may have been part of the initial expansion, while the Faraoskop skeleton, dated to 2 000 years ago, could have been part of the second expansion. If the latter is true, then it could coincide with the idea of shellfish collectors coming from East Africa before 2 000 years ago (see Chapter 7). Faraoskop is only 30 kilometres inland from the mega-middens at Lamberts Bay on the Cape West Coast. We should also recognise, however, that the haplogroup LOd1b2b is widespread among northern Kalahari hunters (see Table 8.2), so expansion this far south appears to be very unusual and may support the hypothesis of the connection to the shellfish collectors.

Expansion from East to southern Africa

The movement of domestic stock from East to southern Africa would have been facilitated by the grasslands to the southeast of Lake Victoria (Chritz et al. 2015), which connected to the tsetse-free corridor linking Tanzania with the northern Kalahari (Figure 5.1), This migration route was anticipated almost a century ago by Schapera (1930: 24–25), who observed:

> The East African highlands are connected with the south by a favourable route passing between the escarpments in the east ... and the elevated ridges and plateaus of Central Africa ... to the diversified plateau between Lakes Nyasa and Bangweolo and the Zambesi River.
>
> This diversified plateau is important as the central point from which migration routes branch out into South Africa ... The high steppes afford the best pasture and facilitate movement, and in addition are more healthy for men and animals than the low-lying coastlands or the moister portions of the interior with their malaria, tsetse fly and other infectious diseases ... Hence invading peoples must either wipe out their predecessors completely or live side by side with them, the latter a condition likely to result in intermingling and the formation of hybrid races and cultures.

Schapera was still writing in the period of the Hamitic Hypothesis, which equated the 'Hottentots' with the people of ancient Egypt (Morris 2014), so he was looking for contacts further north in Africa.

156

Although the Hamitic Hypothesis is no longer seen as tenable, both the genomics and linguistics are strong evidence of contact between East and southern Africa at least by 2 000 years ago, and possibly even earlier. The lactase persistence gene came southward from East African herders. The LOd1b2b1b mtDNA from Faraoskop (see Table 8.1) shows a link with Fingira in Malawi, but separated by 3 000 years. Although it may not appear so at first glance, a more important connection might be that between the burial of the young girl from Kasteelberg, dated to 1300 BP, and the skeleton from Luxmanda, dated to 3000 BP. The LOd1a1a reading from Kasteelberg is of the southern Bushman type, but she also shares 40 per cent of her genome with the Luxmanda skeleton, which is both East African and Levantine in its origin (Skoglund et al. 2017). Why does the girl have southern Bushman genomics and why was she buried in a pastoralist site? She obviously had Bushman genes, but still had a genetic connection with herders from East Africa. The most logical answer would be that somewhere in her ancestry were people from East Africa who had intermarried with local hunters. Like Barbieri et al. (2014), I would suggest that incoming pastoralist males bringing their stock from East Africa took local wives. Without repeated input of mtDNA from East Africa, the southern African genomes dominated.

Table 8.2 shows the results of the collection of genomic data in the Kalahari by Mark Stoneking's group. The columns show the number of individuals sampled (n) and the percentage of that particular genome within the sampled group. Here we can see the distinct north/south separation between the mtDNA (female) Southern Bushman line, LOd1a1a (that is,

157

Table 8.2: Genomic table of modern Kalahari populations

n	Population	LOd1a1a	LOd1b2b
14	≠Hoan	14.28571	0
31	G/wi	9.677419	0
29	Nama	6.896552	13.7931
40	Ju/'hoan North	0	35
51	Hei//om	0	21.56863
31	Ta'a West	0	16.12903
19	Kgalagadi	0	15.78947
35	Nharo	0	11.42857
44	Ju/'hoan South	0	11.36364
15	G//ana	0	6.666667
30	Herero	0	6.666667
17	Kalanga	0	5.882353
42	Shua	0	4.761905
27	!Xuun	0	3.703704
30	Ta'a East	0	3.333333
38	Damara	0	2.631579
32	//AniBuga	0	0
11	BntNAMmix	0	0
21	Himba	0	0
20	Mbukushu	0	0
25	Ta'a North	0	0
22	Tshwa	0	0
17	Tswana	0	0
17	!Xo	0	0

n	Population	A3b1
21	Nharo	42.86
37	Hei//om	37.84
25	!Xuun	32
28	Nama	28.57
30	Ju/'hoan_South	23.33
22	Ju/'hoan_North	22.73
31	Ta'a_West	22.58
24	//AniBuga	20.83
20	!Xo	20
15	Tshwa	13.33
29	Herero	10.34
21	Kgalagadi	9.52
21	Ta'a_East	9.52
36	Damara	8.33
24	Shua	8.33
18	G/wi	5.56
23	Ta'a_North	4.35
21	Himba	0
19	Kalanga	0
12	Mbukushu	0
20	Owambo	0
18	Tswana	0
19	G//ana	0
13	≠Hoan	0

Source: Mark Stoneking, personal communication.

those who are based in southern Namibia and South Africa), and both Kalahari Khoisan and Bantu-speakers who do not show this genome. The Kalahari Khoisan (Bushman and Khoe) genome LOd1b2b is quite different, but exhibits admixture with some Bantu-speakers, such as Herero, but others, such as Mbukushu and Tswana, are exempted. The NRY-chromosome (male) genomics show the admixture between men among the Khoisan and some Bantu-speaking populations. The outcome of this important study is to show the separation among women of the Southern Bushmen groups from those in the northern Kalahari. This also underlines the linguistic distinction between the northern Kx'a-speakers, and southern Tuu-speakers described above.

The mtDNA genomic signature of LOd1b2b is widely dispersed throughout the northern Kalahari, as seen in Table 8.2. Moreover, it differs markedly from the distribution of the southern Bushman signature of LOd1a1a (the same as the young girl from Kasteelberg) and includes Bushmen from the more southerly areas of Botswana (G/wi from the Central Kalahari Game Reserve, and ≠Hoan from south of the reserve). Only the Nama exhibit both. Why the Nama should be different may be due to their history, which indicates that they moved northward from South Africa and dominated the Damara, who lived in northern Namibia. This would also account for the discrepancy in Uren et al. (2016: Table 1), which shows LOd1b2b missing from their Nama sample. This may have been taken around the Orange/Gariep River, on the boundary between Namibia and South Africa, where the genomic history is slightly different from that in the northern Kalahari.

160

Palaeo-climatic variables

As noted before, the two Bushman languages, Kx'a (Ju) and Tuu, are so different that speakers of one cannot understand the other. Since at their margins they are separated by only 150 kilometres, this is indeed surprising. Mechanisms for this separation still have to be worked out, and thus far the archaeological record is of little help, since mostly all we have to work with is the distribution of stone tools (Sadr 2015). These can be fitted within known palaeo-environmental conditions, but they also still need fine-tuning and dating. The geneticists have estimated that the separation between the two linguistic groups is an old one and may go back as far as 30 000 years (Pickrell et al. 2012). This would coincide with a drier period 33 000 to 23 000 years ago, as seen in the environmental evidence from Wonderwerk Cave along the southern margin of the Kalahari (Brook et al. 2010). This may have depopulated the interior of this part of southern Africa, forcing different groups apart.

There is a great deal of variability across the subcontinent and discussion about how to interpret the palaeo-environmental conditions at the local level. As Chevalier and Chase (2015: 117) say: 'Late Quaternary climate variability in the southern African tropics is still only poorly resolved.' They go on to say that temperature differences between the LGM, around 18 000 BP, and the Holocene could have been as much as 6°C, as amplitudes increased with distance from the coast. This may indicate another time of stress, when the interior of southern Africa was sparsely populated, as evidenced by the low number of archaeological sites found (Mitchell 2002: 109).

Such conditions would have encouraged people to migrate to the coast to avoid the extremes. There they would have had access to the coastal shelf off the South Coast when sea levels were as much as 130 metres below present levels. Old lineages that may have separated around the time of the LGM are LOd2c, LOd1b and LOd1c (Morris et al. 2014).

Another palaeo-environmental database comes from the analysis of fine-grained pollen from dassie middens. Some excellent results suggest that between 6000 and 1000 BP, northern Namibia experienced wetter conditions than the present (Gil-Romera et al. 2006). Thus, we have an indicator that supports what Shaw et al. (2003) have said about the period around 2500 BP in the northern Kalahari, which would have been favourable for good grazing and welcomed the earliest pastoralists coming down the tsetse-free corridor.

The warm period around 1000 BP increased precipitation in the summer-rainfall areas of southern Africa, creating micro-environments conducive to expanded agro-pastoralism. This occurred at the same time that humped zebu cattle (*Bos indicus*) from the Indian subcontinent were cross-bred with African taurine cattle (*Bos taurus*), resulting in hybrids well adapted to the warm African climate. Expansion to southern Africa vastly increased herds during the Later Iron Age. This was also when the hiatus of occupation of Kasteelberg took place, and when cattle entered the southwestern Cape in numbers we associate with the Khoekhoe herds.

Four periods of development

We might suggest four different periods of herder development in southern Africa. In the first period, hunter-fisher shellfish collectors speaking an East-African-related language, perhaps similar to Sandawe hunters, who speak a click language, may have been the first migrants moving south, opening up an avenue along the river systems of Zambia, the Zambezi and northern Kalahari parallelling the tsetse-free corridor between 3 000 and 2 000 years ago. These migrants went on to exploit the rich coastal resources on the West Coast and, if they were mostly males, to introduce the Y-chromosome A1b1b2, but followed closely with the arrival of the genetic signature of LOd1b2b.

In the second period, the first pastoralists speaking a Khoe-Kwadi language entered southern Africa around 2 000 years ago, primarily with flocks of sheep, moving along the rivers, down the West Coast to the Cape, where they may have introduced the LOd1b2b signature. Their pottery was undecorated, black burnished ware, as seen at Die Kelders.

The third period was during the first millennium AD, when these herders took wives from the local hunting groups of the Cape, resulting in the LOd1a1a signature. Today only the Nama have both LOd1a1a and LOd1b2b genes (see Table 8.2). They also used spouted ceramics.

The fourth period of herder development came after these herders were established at the Cape, at the beginning of the second millennium AD. There was contact with Bantu-speakers in the Eastern Cape from whom they obtained the cattle in numbers first seen by the earliest Portuguese explorers at the end of the 15th century. These were the Khoekhoen. Khoekhoe language developed and spread northwards into Namibia with the Nama, who dominated the Damara. Lugged pottery was developed at this time.

If this model is correct, then the 1000 BP changes towards cattle herding would also have put pressure on local hunting (Sonqua) communities. Cattle ownership would have widened the gap between hunters and herders, pushing the foragers even further to the bottom of the hierarchy. This could be the reason for the meaning of 'Khoekhoe = people-people' or 'real people', not to be confused with 'Sonqua', or people without stock living off the bush.

As a postscript to this model of the earliest history of contact between East and southern Africa, there is one major drawback: no early pottery has been recognised from the mega-middens of the Cape, and there is debate on how pottery arrived at the Cape (Sadr & Sampson 2006). If the model offered here is correct, then the lack of early pottery would be surprising, since the Kansyore hunter-fishers had been pottery makers for thousands of years before domestic animals even reached East Africa. One reason for the lacuna in the Western Cape might be the current paradigm, which only admits to pottery arriving at the Cape 2 000 years ago. On this assumption, any small pieces of pottery in the mega-middens might just be ignored, or be seen as having been pushed down from the surface. This is the argument Jerardino and Yates (1996: 10) use to explain the appearance of sheep bones below the surface levels at Steenbokfontein Cave, situated inland on the West Coast close to the mega-middens at Lamberts Bay: 'The sheep remains (*Ovis aries*) in Layer 1 and 2 are likely to be intrusive from deposits above.' If the initial incoming people had been small groups of men, then pottery could have been limited, and small fragments difficult to place in their correct provenance in the large shell middens. This would mean that contact with East Africa was much earlier than previously accepted.

CHAPTER 9

Where Are the Khoisan Today?

The San or Bushmen hunter-gatherers of southern Africa offer good examples of foraging peoples. Some of these, such as the Ju/'hoansi Bushmen of Nyae Nyae in Namibia, have been intensively studied by anthropologists (for example, Marshall 1976; Lee 1979), so we know a lot about how they lived until very recently. In fact, so well-known have they become that these people living in the Kalahari Desert are often seen as archetypical examples of hunting societies. This is typified by the famous film by John Marshall, *The Hunters* (1957), which depicted a giraffe hunt. The film was widely shown to anthropology students, including those in the United States, and made ≠Toma, the lead hunter in the film, the face of Nyae Nyae to the world (Figures 9.1 and 9.2).

We must be wary of such generalisations, particularly since we know from both archaeology and the historical record that all parts of southern Africa, from the coast to the interior, were occupied by hunters in the past. Each ecological zone would have required adjustment to its own peculiarities, with the result that there would have been a great deal of variation among these hunting peoples.

Figure 9.1: ≠Toma, the lead hunter in John Marshall's film *The Hunters* (Marshall & Ritchie 1984; see also Thomas 1969).

Figure 9.2: ≠Toma in his mealie field in Nyae Nyae a few months before he died (Andrew Smith).

Unfortunately (or perhaps we should say inevitably), the outside world has impinged upon the last surviving hunting groups today, so they have adapted to the pressures placed upon them. Adjustment to these outside pressures has included schools for their children, dealing with tourists, and perhaps also having small herds of cattle or goats, all of which have become needed in order to find alternative ways of living that will bring an income to buy the things they have become accustomed to: sugar, tea, tobacco, maize meal, etc.

A number of groups, such as the Working Group of Indigenous Minorities in Southern Africa (WIMSA) and the South African San Institute (SASI), along with Survival International, have tried to intervene on behalf of the Bushmen in the Kalahari as more powerful political groups have pushed them aside and off their traditional hunting territories. There

Figure 9.3: Ju/'hoansi at Nyae Nyae Pans setting off to hunt and forage during the 1980s (Andrew Smith).

Figure 9.4: A recent photo of a Ju/'hoansi hunter preparing his poison arrows (Andrew Smith).

169

is a tendency in the corridors of power in Windhoek and Gaborone to ignore the needs of people at the very bottom of the social ladder. Le Roux and White (2004) bring together numerous interviews with San people, across eight language groups; the voices they include are of younger people asking questions of their elders, and being willing to use their education to understand how the Bushmen lived (and how many would still like to live). As Suzman (2017: 94) says: '[F]ewer than one in ten Nyae Nyae Ju/'hoansi interviewed in 2010 … considered farming to be an important food source' (Figures 9.3 and 9.4).

Namibia

The Nyae Nyae Farmers' Cooperative (NNFC) was set up in Namibia during the 1980s with funds acquired by John Marshall and his colleagues. This was an attempt to allow local Ju/'hoansi hunters access to the means to become cattle keepers, which included giving them stock and help with building lion-proof kraals (Marshall & Ritchie 1984). The exercise was initially quite successful (Figure 9.5), since many hunters had worked as stockmen in the past, but only as long as funds were available, especially to build lion-proof enclosures. In the 1990s, a change in emphasis from the outside (the source of the funding) led to the cattle programme being gradually reduced. This example shows how dependent the Bushmen had become on external philosophies of where their future lay. The new direction wanted the Bushman traditional hunting life to continue, and not to be diluted

Figure 9.5: Ju/'hoansi man milking one of his cows, Nyae Nyae, 1986 (Andrew Smith).

by ideas of domestication. There is no question that in becoming herders they would be less likely to pass on their tracking/hunting skills to their children, but tracking today only has a limited future for a narrow tourist or commercial hunting market. As it is, there is a significant threat from other African herders, such as the Herero, moving with their stock into the hunters' lands, and the Bushmen becoming more and more marginalised.

Bushman representatives have become part of the modern state of Namibia, so they have some voice in parliament, but the concept of 'leadership' among the Bushmen is highly contentious. Because no one is seen as being above anyone else in Bushmen culture, outsiders often have been the ones to define direction and to make decisions. Pressures from the outside to

171

accommodate what is seen as the need for Bushmen to adjust have had a downside. The introduction of new technologies, alien to Bushman culture, and the assumptions built into these, without any real understanding of what the outcomes might be, have also not helped. For example, the NNFC were given small trucks to facilitate the movement of goods needed by the community, but some of the drivers got drunk and wrecked the vehicles.

Alcohol is a major problem, as it is among many of the world's first peoples who feel marginalised. There was little alcohol in Nyae Nyae until the 1980s, during the Border War. Bottle stores opened up in Tsumkwe, the administrative centre of Bushmanland, Namibia, and the soldiers had money to spend. After the war, the soldiers went away, but the bottle stores stayed.

The tracking skills of the Bushmen led to many finding employment in the army. Their ability to read sign under very difficult conditions is phenomenal but requires consistent learning from a very young age. Unfortunately, formal schooling interferes with bush learning at a critical time in a young person's life. Some fathers are still very keen to teach their sons how to track, and, in my experience with these young people, those who do learn are very aware of the environment, and are usually the ones to see the game animals first.

Botswana

The Central Kalahari Game Reserve (CKGR) was set up in the 1960s by Sir Seretse Khama, the first president of inde-

172

pendent Botswana, as an area where Bushmen could live and practise their hunting-and-gathering way of life. In the 1980s, however, the government of Botswana decreed that the life of the Bushmen was an anachronism in the modern world, and the Bushmen had to be settled so that their children could go to school and the people become members of the modern state. This decree, however, occurred when Tswana stock owners, benefiting from the country's diamond wealth, had built up large cattle holdings and were looking for new pastures. Boreholes were dug in outlying areas to provide water for the herds, and this coincided with the discovery of diamonds in the CKGR. One might suggest that preventing the Bushmen from having any rights within the reserve would be advantageous to the Tswana leadership once exploitation of the diamonds began.

The bottom line is that the Bushmen have been isolated in small villages on the edge of the CKGR. There is little work to be had, so the people have had to subsist on hand-outs from the government and ennui has set in. Matters were exacerbated when a bottle store was opened in one of the lodges, and alcoholism became rife among the population. It is very difficult for Bushmen fathers to lead their children to learn bush skills under these conditions, so, as in Namibia, there is a great loss of skills and expertise.

Numerous attempts have been made, with the help of Survival International, to allow the Bushmen to return to the CKGR, and ultimately they won a court case in 2006 to permit this. The Botswana government has blocked this court decision at all levels, and a number of Bushmen who tried to return were jailed for trespassing and badly maltreated by the police.

South Africa

The descendants of Khoisan peoples of South Africa are very easy to find, as under the old apartheid classification system they were designated 'Coloureds', or people assumed to be of mixed ancestry. Of course, this had to be a generalisation, as many rural folk could well trace their Khoisan lineage directly without any admixture from the outside. An example could be the Karretjiemense of the Karoo, who are descendants from hunters like the /Xam of the Bleek and Lloyd archive (De Jongh 2012). Other examples could be the ≠Khomani, who live north of the Orange/Gariep River and whose hunting territory would have included the Kgalagadi Transfrontier Park. Their land was restored as a result of their exclusion from the former Kalahari Gemsbok National Park under apartheid. However, to achieve the necessary numbers for this restitution, outsiders had to be included. These were people whose families had weaker ties with the area of the national park, probably including descendants of the Korana. The Korana were Khoekhoen who lived along the Gariep (but who could have included refugees from the smallpox epidemic of the early 18th century) until they were forced off their pasture territories by the expanding colony in the second half of the 19th century. They either moved north, away from the river, to join the hunters or became labourers on the colonial farms.

The result of turmoil, including two Korana Wars along the Gariep (Strauss 1979), has been language loss and incorporation into the social and religious life of modern South Africa, with only a handful of older women still able to converse in their original //Ng language. All others use Afrikaans as their language. In spite of this disruptive history, there is a surprising continuity in stories retained among the farm workers of the Karoo. This is seen in the similarity of the stories told to Wilhelm Bleek and Lucy Lloyd in their Mowbray home in the 19th century (Bleek & Lloyd 1911), and in the work done by José Manuel de Prada-Samper (2016) in interviewing and taping their Khoisan descendants in various places across the Karoo.

Historical attempts to 'pacify' the Bushmen go back to the first British occupation of the Cape when Lord Macartney, the governor, gave small stock to the Sneeuberg Bushmen in 1798 (Boucher & Penn 1992: 178) with the assumption that they would become herders. This stopped the raiding of the colonists' herds for some time, but the Bushmen had no intention of abandoning their hunting lifestyle. They accepted the animals gladly, then proceeded to eat them. Monica Wilson (1969: 71–72) notes that this 'indeed reduced raiding for a time, and [local magistrate Andries] Stockenström noted with satisfaction in 1820 that some San had taken to stock-breeding, but few bands of hunters – other than those attached to mission stations or a group of herders – seem to have transformed into herders … The transformation of hunter to herder involves a radical shift in values, in particular the willingness to forgo immediate food in order to preserve breeding stock for future supply. Hunters were likely to eat all the stock they acquired.'

The voiceless Khoisan

Oral traditions work well in small-scale societies. However, working with a wider world brings the need for greater communication. The hunters and herders of southern Africa had no written language, thus they tended not to be understood by colonial people, most of whom probably did not care. As happened all over the world, indigenous people were forced aside (see the Australian Aboriginal example in Trudgen 2000), to be placed at the bottom of the social hierarchy.

The result of this has meant that until recently there has been no indigenous voice, although Le Roux and White (2004) have recognised this and tried to rectify the lacuna. Almost everything we know about southern Africa's first people has been filtered through a colonial (and often prejudiced) prism. In other words, hunters and herders cannot speak for themselves. This is done by outside observers. Even when there have been Khoisan descendants who are literate, they write in the language of the colonisers, which means there can be a dislocation between the First Nations view of the world and how it expresses itself, in contrast to how outsiders think.

A good example would be hunters who can read spoor the way outsiders read a book (Stander et al. 1997). The language of the track requires getting very close to the animal's behaviour, in fact almost becoming the animal. The result is a spiritual rapport with animals. A successful hunter has respect for his prey animals and their place in the wider landscape. The language of the hunters, both vocal and sign, is an easy communication because they all deal with this view of the world. These aspects of hunter life are not easily understood by outside observers, no matter how empathetic they might be. To fully understand, any outsider would have to learn to speak the language of the hunters.

In the experience of working with hunter-gatherers, the

colonial filters and language can take on new meanings for outside observers. An example is Myburgh's (2013) story of how he tries to become a Bushman by living with them for a long time. He appears not to have been able to speak their language, so has to use the interpretations of others to express what he thinks his G/wi informants believe, and quotes //Kabbo, /Han≠kasso and others from Bleek and Lloyd's *Specimens of Bushman Folklore* (1911). He uses his experiences as a personal spiritual odyssey.

The Bleek and Lloyd archive (Skotnes 2007) has given us a reference point against which we can compare the historical development of stories, even when the language has changed from the /Xam of their informants to the Afrikaans spoken by the descendants of the hunter-gatherers still living in Bushman-land and the Karoo (De Prada-Samper 2016). While the stories connect with the past, the storytellers are not 'Bushmen', and do not have the experience of living in the environment as foragers. The descendants have survived by acculturation, both social and linguistic, into the dominant society, albeit still at the lower levels. The spirituality of the stories still resonates with the past, even if the storytellers' world has been moderated by Christianity over the past 150 years.

The Bleek and Lloyd archive shows how much has been lost when language disappears. Only a few older people still have knowledge of //Ng, a Tuu or !Ui language that would have been widely spoken by Sonqua in the Northern Cape. All other dialects of South African Tuu-speakers have virtually gone extinct.

Attempts to keep Khoisan traditions alive do happen but in widely dispersed communities. Historically, these have revolved around mission stations set up by foreign missionaries, such as the Moravian Church or the London Missionary Society in the late 18th and early 19th centuries. The church centre is still very important, as we see in Genadendal in the Western Cape. Young people have become interested in traditional rëel dancing, and competitions are held between different communities. The real problem is that the stories, the knowledge of plant use and the understanding of how one lives in the dry lands of South Africa is knowledge held by the older generation, and with their passing comes a huge loss.

The descendants of the Khoisan are the most marginalised people in South Africa, as typified by the Karretjiemense of the Karoo. These people are some of the last remnants of the /Xam Bushmen who survived until the end of the 19th century as hunter-gatherers, albeit under enormous pressure to become virtual slave labour for the expanding colonial frontier. The Karretjiemense adapted to become nomadic sheep-shearers when the merino wool boom benefited (mostly) white farmers across the Karoo in the early 20th century. They had no resources and, being illiterate, no way to organise themselves as sheep farmers in their own right, so were pushed to the periphery. Even that became difficult when competition for sheep-shearing labour expanded to include people coming into the area who would work as temporary labour before returning in the off season back to where they came from (often not the Karoo).

In his book on the Karretjiemense, De Jongh eloquently phrases this loss: 'The Karretjie People are still scattered across a vast area, sedentary or moving in small groups, are generally illiterate, have a limited range of skills and are devoid of significant resources.' They are increasingly forced by competition to live a more sedentary life in poor settlements on the outskirts of towns, But this 'will thrust their outcast and debilitated status in their faces … [as] people who find themselves effectively strangers in the land, confined to road verges, debarred from private property, subject to insult and humiliation, and forced to trek in search of a meagre subsistence … they signal that they are strangers in the land, but also their understanding that they are strangers in what should be their *own* land' (De Jongh 2012: 168–169).

The night sky

In the middle of the Karoo, where the skies are clearest, a new radio telescope is being built. The Square Kilometre Array (SKA) is an international project that will put South Africa at the forefront of modern astronomy. But these modern star-watchers will not be the first in the Karoo. Astronomers and archaeologists are increasingly recognising that the Bushmen, some of the world's earliest humans, were also in tune with the seasons, and aware of the changes in the night skies. But even with the efforts by the scientists of the SKA project to be inclusive, the San Council objects to their presence, as they are considered outsiders, and therefore should not have a voice.

Such problems are not unique to South Africa. In Uganda, according to Oruru et al. (2020), 'one of the greatest challenges of most African astronomers today is being able to make local African world views more scientific, to link them to other

179

world views, and to demystify the mysterious heavenly bodies of antiquity'. The authors state that one of the strategies for trying to bridge the gap between traditional and modern astronomy is to reinterpret myths using the scientific lens of modern astronomy. This can show that scientific reasoning is not something new and not divorced from our life and culture.

Again, the encounter between science and the indigenous world is fraught with lack of understanding on both sides. This only changes when First Nations people fully understand how science can benefit them, as can be seen among Native Americans who eventually saw how genetics could be used to support their claims to territory and resources. In fact, in South Africa it was with the help of historians, anthropologists and archaeologists that the Richtersveld claimants won their 2001 case against Alexkor mine in both Constitutional Court and Supreme Court of Appeal judgments.

Among the G/wi of the central Kalahari, 'N!adima is the giver of life … All are his creatures, which he suffers to exist for as long as he chooses, leading the style of life that he ordained for them and making use of what he has made available to them' (Silberbauer 1981: 53). 'The Milky Way is one of the paths along which N!adima carries the sun' (Ibid: 108):

> [W]hen the Milky Way stands upon the earth, the Milky Way turns across in front while the Milky Way means to wait, while the Milky Way feels the stars are turning back; while the stars feel that the sun is the one who has turned back; he is upon his path; the stars turn back; while they go to fetch the dawn; that they may lie nicely, while the Milky Way lies nicely. (Watson 1991: 12)

Both the Nharo, of the Ghanzi district of Botswana, and the Auen, also known as //kau //en, the northerly neighbours of the Nharo, believe that the moon is an old man, and a rain-giver, while the sun is a young girl. They are also aware that the path of the sun is shorter in winter. Stars are seasonal indicators among the Nharo, who have three seasons: spring, summer and winter. They also have names for the constellations: the Pointers to the Southern Cross are male lions, and Orion is a female hartebeest (see Schapera 1930: 218; and also Silberbauer 1981: 109 for the G/wi).

Fish traps

There has been an assumption that the stone-walled tidal fish traps of the Cape South Coast were built by coastal-foraging Khoisan. Attempts by archaeologists to find fish bones on shell middens close to these traps near Still Bay have proved futile (Hine et al. 2010). Such traps were known to have been used and rebuilt in the 19th and 20th centuries, but they were more likely to have been colonial constructions used by farm labourers when they brought the cattle herds from the interior to the coast to allow them to forage on seaweed. The traps could well have been ways of improving the efficiency of tidal pools known to coastal foragers, but we would have expected any fish caught to have been processed nearby on the coast, and at least some of the bones of their catches to be included in archaeological material found on neighbouring shell middens.

CHAPTER 10

How Did the Khoisan Lose Their History?

In this, the third decade of the 21st century, the COVID-19 pandemic has forced many countries and societies to rethink much of the economic and social disparities that exist throughout the world. This, of course, equally pertains to the descendants of the Khoisan, whose history tends to be ignored today. The omission may be because they were displaced more than 300 years ago, but it was also exacerbated by apartheid, which pushed people of different groups into a single category called 'Coloured'. The pandemic has not only highlighted wealth difference but has also, along with awareness of police brutality against people of 'colour', led to worldwide protest. Is it now time to recognise the antecedents of everyone? Perhaps we have an opportunity to show that whatever one's background, whether slave, native or colonial, everyone has something to add to the modern mix.

One example of this need to rethink is the removal of statues of people with questionable pasts, which has been of burning importance in recent years. While not everyone agreed with the removal of the statue of Cecil Rhodes from the UCT campus in April 2015, for many members of the UCT community Rhodes was a symbol of South Africa's objectionable history, which led to apartheid. However, the land on which the university is built, close to the main Rhodes Memorial, came from his bequest, and the statue of Rhodes sat on the steps above the rugby field for many years without comment from the student body. But the demographics of the university have shifted. The 'Rhodes Must Fall' movement has brought history to the fore, not only in South Africa but also at Oxford University's Oriel College, where another statue commemorates Rhodes and the scholarships for exceptional students that his great wealth endowed.

The effects of colonisation

All over the world, hunter-gatherers have tended to be pushed to the periphery of farming societies. This was probably the case with the expansion of agriculture out of the Near East into Europe 9 000 years ago (Gronenborn 2004), and with the growth of pastoralism across the Sahara shortly thereafter (Di Lernia 1999). It is not always easy to know what happened to the hunters once they were in the ambit of food producers, but if what happened in southern Africa is anything to go by, the hunters were either incorporated into farming (Bantu-speaking) societies, usually by hypergyny (one-way gene flow), with males taking Bushman wives (the hunters could seldom have the bride-wealth payments for them to have farmer wives), or pushed into the mountains where they could still hunt. When Archbishop Desmond Tutu had his complete

183

genome sequenced, he found he was half Bushman (Schuster et al. 2010). This was no surprise, as Tobias (1974: Figure 1.7) had already shown the degree of admixture of southern African Bantu-speakers and Bushmen using the serum protein allele Gm 1,13.

I am suggesting here that a similar scenario resulted in the direct ancestors of Khoekhoen: East African male herders taking local Bushman wives, with the hunters yielding the most productive pasture lands. The same thing may have happened to the earliest herders in the eastern part of South Africa. Thin-walled pottery, different from the thick Early Iron Age wares, has been found in KwaZulu-Natal (Mazel 1992). It may have come with early herders, but this is still disputed, because no domestic animals have been found there before the Early Iron Age. This pottery was dominated by Iron Age farmer pottery a couple of centuries later.

The eastern part of South Africa is the summer-rainfall area, good for growing sorghum and millet, the traditional crops of Bantu-speaking farmers. Thus, the summer-rainfall crops limited their westward expansion along the coast of southern Africa, leaving the western half of South Africa, the winter-rainfall area, to the pastoralists. Once European colonists decided that the Cape was a good place for farming, they brought their winter-rainfall crops – wheat, barley, rye, etc. – and the Khoekhoen were pushed to the periphery.

In any colonisation exercise, farmers are inevitably the more powerful since they congregate in larger groups, which can be fed by the products of their fields. The difference between the settlement of Bantu-speaking farmers and European colonists in southern Africa was one of race. The Africans did not mind taking hunter-gatherer wives and making them full members of their society. In contrast, although the Dutch treated the Khoisan as subhuman, and this continued well into the 20th century (Dubow 1995), farmers were not reluctant to have them as concubines, resulting in mixed-race children, but to marry a Khoisan woman was outside the acceptable norms of this society.

Several important points are made by Brink (2004) in relation to early colonisation. The first is that the original Dutch governor at the Cape, Jan van Riebeeck, was given explicit instructions by the Heeren XVII in Amsterdam before his departure in 1651 not to 'injure' the local natives or their cattle. The second was that he was to identify arable lands close to the refreshment station he was to set up, and to map them as proof of possession. These two injunctions were at odds with each other. 'Injury' was meant physically, but there was no concept in Dutch society that land should not be bounded and fenced – a complete disaster to transhumant pastoralists. Equally, cattle were not just 'meat' to the Khoekhoen, as they were for the Dutch. The animals meant status and identity, giving place socially and psychologically to allow the owner to lead in political negotiation.

How the Dutch managed this was through the written record (Brink 2004). The VOC required an oath of allegiance to be sworn, which would exclude outsiders such as the Khoe, drawing a clear line between 'civilised' and 'savage' people. Documentation supported the Dutch enterprise, and no illiterate Khoe could dispute these legal exercises, as no lawyers would have taken their case. When Van Riebeeck was recalled from Tonkin, following the accusation that he was lining his pockets while in charge of the VOC trading station there, it was probably a resort to law that allowed him to be reinstated into the VOC. Indeed, it was during his return voyage from Vietnam that he spent 18 days at Table Bay and saw its potential. This made him the ideal candidate to set up the refreshment station when the idea was proposed in 1651.

The result, as we know, was to completely disrupt Khoe society, and to cause a reaction against this theft of land and property. But to no avail. The Khoe lost the two wars against the Dutch colony and were ultimately forced into servitude. Had the Khoe killed some Dutch, instead of just stealing their cattle, the outcome might have been very different – as it was when the Khoe killed Francisco de Almeida and many of his men in 1510, with the result that the Portuguese avoided the Cape for decades. The Khoe dealt with the Dutch as they traditionally dealt with their enemies – by raiding for cattle. They had no understanding of what kind of society supported Dutch mercantile aspirations.

Up until 1713, the Khoe were able to sell their labour to colonial farmers, moving between jobs. After the smallpox epidemic of 1713 many of those Khoe who survived were frightened away from the colony at Table Bay. Although previously there had been legal protection against enslavement, the epidemic caused such a severe shortage of labour that this was ignored, and the status of the Khoe (native labour) became similar to that of slaves. The reason offered was that the colonial farmers were rearing their children, so should have some return. This resulted in 'enserfment' (control over where the Khoe were able to live and work), informally before 1721, formally after 1775 (Shell 1994: 27–30). The emancipation of both slaves and Khoekhoen between 1828 and 1838 was one of the main reasons for the exodus of the trekboers from the Cape Colony in 1836. In 1848, the English naturalist John Leyland, travelling north of the Orange/Gariep River, observed: 'A large proportion of them (boers) are persons that have gone from the authority of British law ... their object being to treat the Bechuanas as slaves, in which position the Hottentots were previous to the English taking possession of the Cape' (Leyland 1866: 58).

Bushman resistance to colonial expansion

One area where Bushmen initially were successful in preventing colonial expansion into their territories was on the northern frontier, south of the Orange/Gariep River. In spite of a resolution of February 1770 by the VOC governor that was meant to restrict the colonists from pushing into the area north of Graaff-Reinet, by 1775 it was obvious that the farmers were not paying any heed to this (Moodie 1838–1842, Part III: 46, 48). The colonists were expanding northwards and putting pressure on the Bushmen of the Sneeuberg by killing off the game that had been plentiful in the area. As Sampson (1988: 38) says of the lower Seekoei Valley: 'By all accounts the flats were inhabited by enormous, dense herds of herbivores in the late 1700s and early 1800s', including wildebeest, zebra, springbok and blesbok. But the Bushmen were pushing back, and so effective was their resistance that Field Cornet Adriaan van Jaarsveld organised a commando to try to recoup stock losses by the colonists in 1775.

In 1777, Colonel Robert Gordon was sufficiently disturbed by Van Jaarsveld's report, which said that around 240 Bushmen had been killed (Cullinan 1992: 37), to go and see for himself what was happening in the lower Seekoei Valley. Gordon's expedition reached a point about 80 kilometres south of the Orange/Gariep River before turning back. The reason given for turning back and not going on to the river was that the farmers he was travelling with were afraid of the Bushmen and would not go any further. On this first trip beyond the Sneeuberg, Gordon was unable to meet the Bushmen. They fled any time he got close. The following year, accompanied by Governor Joachim van Plettenberg, he tried again, but with no success. In his journal entry for 13 November 1777, he quotes Chief Koerekei's shouting from a mountain: 'What are you doing on my land? You have taken all the places where the eland and other game live. Why did you not stay where the sun goes down, where you first came from?' In response to the question why he could not live in peace with the boers, Koerekei responded that he did not want to lose the country where he was born (Cullinan 1992: 35).

Van Plettenberg set up a stone beacon at the point where they turned back, in the same area that Gordon had retreated in 1777. The Van Plettenberg beacon became a landmark for later travellers, such as Barrow (1801, 1804), who visited it in October 1797, as it was supposed to designate the northern boundary of the colony. But again it was of no avail. Expanding colonist use of the territory meant increasing pressure on land and resources, and greater theft of stock by the Bushmen. This resulted in commandos being organised against the hunters, not only to retrieve stolen stock but also to kill the hunters.

188

By 1786 the commandos had killed so many Bushmen that the colonists were able to spread north of the Orange River in search of pasture for their stock, and the Sneeuberg was included in the new district of Graaff-Reinet.

Although the *veldwagtmeester* (field guard) of each district was allowed to organise formally recognised commandos for reprisal raids, the farmers often just took it upon themselves to chase after the thieves. An estimated 2 504 Bushmen were killed between 1788 and 1795, with five commandos being organised in 1787 alone (Newton-King 1986). These, however, were probably only the formal counts. Many more were killed by farmers chasing robbers. Often it was just the men who were killed. Women and children were taken prisoner and distributed among the farmers as virtual slaves (Adhikari 2010).

By 1780 many disenchanted Khoisan defected from service with the colonists, and these people took with them firearms, which they could use effectively. This led to the formation of predatory bands, called Oorlams, under leaders such as Jager Afrikaner, who were able to control large areas of southern Namibia and the northern Cape for many years.

The arrogance of the colonial mentality meant that there was no value given to Bushman society or to their ability to live as hunter-gatherers, except to use their tracking skills, as was the case with farmers who took Khoisan into service. As Colonel Collins wrote, in his journal of a tour of the northeastern boundary in 1809, of the conditions affecting the Bushmen: 'It would be worthy [of] the greatness of the British empire to rescue this unfortunate race from the deplorable state of barbarism to which they have been so long condemned' (Moodie 1838–1842, Part V: 35). He goes on to comment critically on Governor Macartney's attempt to pacify the Bushmen (described in Chapter 3) as a mistaken effort that would never work because they would be unlikely to 'feel all the advantages of permanent establishments and social intercourse' (Ibid: 35) because the missionaries who had tried had failed. Collins stayed over at Genadendal on his return to Cape Town and was pleasantly surprised by the missionaries' success there, but he was unaware that this was among the Khoekhoen of the Sondereind Valley, and not among the Bushmen.

Colonial racial mentality

The separation of people at the Cape has a history as long as the colony itself. We can see this in where people lived, and how they were buried when they died. The excavation at Prestwich Place, a burial site in Cape Town's Green Point district (Malan et al. 2017) showed the disparity. All the 'European' folks who belonged to a church were buried in consecrated cemeteries with walls around them. The rest of the populace was buried elsewhere in the general area of Green Point around the same time, from the mid-18th century onwards. The Prestwich Place burials were outside the formal cemeteries. Thus, only from the conditions of burial and the grave goods have archaeologists been able to separate some of the skeletons. For example, Muslim burials were 'niche' interments, with bodies placed in a niche dug into the side at the bottom of the grave hole, quite different from the rest of the skeletons (Finnegan et al. 2011), while Khoisan burials were upright.

Placing people into a single category meant a great loss,

not only of identity but also of cultural place. This was the fate of the Muslim scholars who came from other countries, such as the Ottoman Empire, to officiate and maintain the faith among people descended from slaves brought in from the Far East and elsewhere in the 17th century. In the narrow world of the Cape social hierarchy, if you were not a member of an established European church, you could not be baptised and therefore would be considered an outcast.

Khoisan, of course, were included in the outcast category, and any semblance of cultural association was quickly sublimated to fit into the perceived needs of the social order separating 'whites' from the rest. Only in places like the mission station at Genadendal were craftsmen trained and given respect, because they learnt to read and write Dutch, and to count (unlike many of the Boers around them). But missionising meant the loss of native lore and the experiences of many people who had lived in southern Africa before colonisation, including much of their oral history. Some remnants of language probably continued for a number of generations, but by 1855, when Governor George Grey visited the mission, he could only find two older men who spoke the Khoe language. The loss was also in the stories and aboriginal skills (such as tracking and hut building, as well as a spiritual place in the landscape, and the burial places of family, all of which disappeared, to be replaced by attempts at acceptance into the colonial world and what it regarded as 'civilised' behaviour.

It was not only in South Africa that this separation happened. We can also see racial separation in Botswana. Under President Ian Khama, the Bushmen have been excluded

191

from the CKGR, which had been set up for them by Khama's father, Sir Seretse Khama, and not allowed to hunt there. The excuse was that the Bushmen needed to be brought into the modern world and no longer be backward. They were forced to settle in small villages on the edge of the reserve, with limited chance of employment and very few resources to raise the quality of their life. Of course, the discovery of diamonds in the reserve had nothing to do with it ...

The 'freak' show, science and ethics

The 'primitive other' has always held a romantic fascination. Whether it was Jean-Jacques Rousseau's idea of 'the noble savage' or the painter Paul Gauguin's sojourn among the Tahitians, colonised people were thought to be 'childlike' in their society and aspirations and thus to be dealt with separately. The other side of the coin was that the historical Khoisan fell into the category of 'slavery', even though enslavement of the native people of the Cape was formally prohibited by the Heeren XVII at the time the VOC colony was set up. But their labour, as far as the Boers were concerned, was no different. A number of examples can be offered to demonstrate how the dominant society at the Cape portrayed those they considered to be unacceptable as equals, without any discussion from the people being portrayed.

The Bushman Diorama: The South African Museum (part of Iziko Museums of South Africa) was historically where the archaeology and ethnology of 'native peoples' was based. This, in part, was due to 19th- and early-20th-century assumptions about the place of indigenous peoples, who were perceived to be the closest to nature and animals. People of more 'sophisticated' cultures, such as the Ancient Egyptians or Chinese, and of course Europeans, were exhibited in the South African Cultural History Museum, housed in the Old Supreme Court Building (now called the Slave Lodge).

Prior to 2001, one of the best known of the exhibits of the South African Museum was the Bushman Diorama. This exhibit purported to show a camp scene in the Kalahari, and featured a group of figures made up by the museum exhibitors from the fine plaster casts in their collection. The diorama was arranged to show how the Bushmen supposedly lived and dressed (Figure 10.1). In fact, it was a composite of a number of different peoples from across southern Africa. These had been cast in the early 20th century by J Drury (Drury & Drennan 1926), who chose them because they were seen as 'typical' Bushmen in appearance, and they conformed to the physical anthropological ideas of the time (Dubow 1995). Nonetheless, visiting the diorama was as close to Bushmen as most South Africans and visitors from overseas ever got, so it was a very popular attraction. For more than 40 years it was called the South African Museum's 'number one drawcard' (Witz et al. 2017a: 184).

By the mid-1990s, with the advent of democracy, the exhibit had become something of an anachronism and the subject of an academic debate. The Bushmen were no longer living as the diorama showed, and the exhibit was seen as immutable and essentialist (unable to change), with no reference to the people cast, or to the conditions under which the

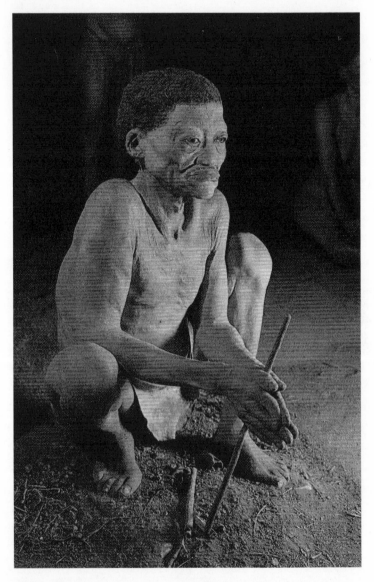

Figure 10.1: Part of the former Bushman Diorama at the
South African Museum (Iziko Museums of South Africa).

casts had been made. As part of broader moves to try to break with some of the racist assumptions of the past, the diorama was closed to the public in April 2001.

But the debate on what the diorama meant to both academics and the general public did not stop there (Davison 2018). The diorama remained in place for 16 years, although not available for viewing (see Witz et al. 2017b), before it was ultimately dismantled, along with other ethnographic displays. In a number of ways this was unfortunate, as the museum could have used the exhibit to show to the public the dreadful history of what had happened to the Bushmen (Adhikari 2010), and the great loss of their language, culture and stories.

Not only did the museum lose a popular attraction, as well as many tour groups because the diorama was no longer on exhibit, but it also lost a real opportunity to be a major player in the discussion around the stereotypes that persist about South Africa's indigenous people, as well as a chance to show what happened to the hunters during the colonial period. This point was made in no uncertain terms by the *Miscast* exhibition at the South African National Gallery in 1996 (Skotnes 1996). When Bushmen visitors who had come to Cape Town for the exhibition and its accompanying conference heard that the Bushman Diorama was being challenged, they said: 'Let us have it. We think it is really fine and would like to display it to our people.' However, following complaints from academics at UCT and the University of the Western Cape about its veracity and value, the diorama remained closed. The Bushman Diorama is one example of where South African institutions have materials at hand that they could effectively use to look at the country's contested past (Witz et al. 2017a).

195

With the removal of the ethnographic displays, we have also lost the punchline of the story of the slightly inebriated woman trying to get up the stairs of a bus in Cape Town while being rudely castigated by the white driver calling her a 'dronk Hotnot'. Her response, when she finally gets to the driver's window to pay her fare, is to rise to her full height (not very tall) and say to him: 'Young man, my ancestors are behind the windows in the museum in the Gardens. Your ancestors stand on the Foreshore, and the seagulls shit on their heads.'

On the N7 highway north of Cape Town, near Yzerfontein, is !Khwa tuu, a museum farm that brings Bushmen from around southern Africa together to train in museum curation and exhibiting collections, as well as in dealing with the public. This centre, with fine exhibits, is filling the gap that the South African Museum could have done in the 1990s. Scientists, as a whole, are often rather poor at portraying their results to a wider public, which allows social media and rumour to fill the gap.

Sara Baartman: During the early British colonial period at the Cape there was considerable public interest in the Khoisan people back in England. This was highlighted by the public display of Sara (Sartjie) Baartman. She was a Khoe woman, probably from a farm east of Jansenville, in the Eastern Cape, who had been recruited to work as a domestic servant in Cape Town. She was induced to go to England by the false promises of a man named Alexander Dunlop, who said she would have a better life there. She travelled to England in 1810 and was exhibited in London as a freak. After touring around England and Ireland, she went on to Paris (Figure 10.2), where she died in 1815. She became internationally famous in Europe as the

'Hottentot Venus'. After her death she was given to Georges Cuvier, of the Muséum d'histoire naturelle in Paris, who wanted to study her anatomy. A moulage (plaster cast) was made of her body before she was dismembered (Fauvelle-Aymar 1999). Her skeleton was on display in the Musée de l'Homme in Paris until the 1970s as an example of skeletal freaks (along with the skeletons of Siamese twins). (I may be the only person today in South Africa to have actually seen her. She was on exhibit at the museum in 1971 when I was working there.)

Sara Baartman was thus known to French museum visitors until 1974, when she was removed from display. In 1994, her skeleton was exhibited at the Musée d'Orsay as part of an exhibition titled *La Sculpture Ethnographique au XIXème Siècle*. The Griqua National Conference was alerted to her existence and it was suggested that she could become a 'possible indigenous people's issue' for Khoisan identity. Discussions between the South African and French governments over her repatriation took place from 1996 to 1998. The French were initially vehemently opposed to her return to South Africa, but ultimately her skeleton was released in 2002 by a unanimous decision of the French National Assembly, which decreed the restitution of Sara Baartman within two months.

With the severing of the French connection, it was up to the South African government to deal with the remains on her return in August 2002. It was decided to create a burial place in Hankey, on the banks of the Gamtoos River, west of Port Elizabeth (today Gqeberha). Not everyone was in total agreement, and various Khoisan groups all had their say in what should happen. No direct descendants were known, although there still are Baartmans in the general area. DNA testing could

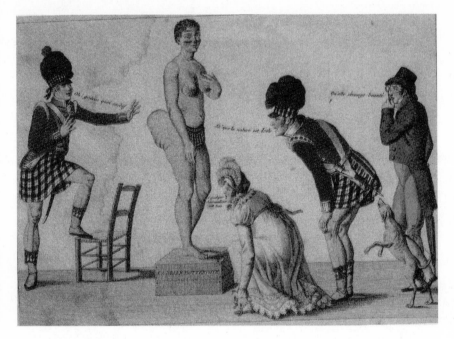

Figure 10.2: Sara Baartman, the 'Hottentot Venus', on display in Paris in 1814 (unattributed cartoon, public domain).

have been used, but this would have been seen as an 'intrusion' by Western science – an anathema to Khoisan activists, who felt she had been badly treated by scientists immediately after her death. The government took charge, and public funds were used for the return of her remains and burial. President Thabo Mbeki officiated at the burial ceremony.

Sara Baartman has become a rather iconic figure in South Africa today. To honour her, the central building on the main campus of UCT, where graduation ceremonies and other important meetings take place, has been renamed Sarah Baartman Hall.

Prestwich Street Burial Ground: We were in similar straits when it came to discuss doing forensic tests on the late-18th- and early-19th-century skeletons from the Prestwich Street burial ground in Cape Town. Over 2 000 skeletons had to be exhumed to make way for a development close to the V&A Waterfront. Everything was recorded by strict archaeological protocols, but again science was seen as intrusive, and a vocal public, who identified with the skeletons as being from Cape Town's lower classes, opposed their detailed study. The skeletons are stored in a specially built ossuary, each in its own box, on the corner of Somerset Road and Buitengracht Street in Cape Town. Because no forensic studies have been permitted, we do not know about the health conditions of people of that class at the time of burial. Demographics have to be gleaned from the way of burial and artefacts associated with each skeleton. Thus, we can separate Muslim from non-Muslim burials and distinguish earlier precolonial Khoisan burials on the site (Finnegan et al. 2011).

From these examples we can see where science falls down in explaining what it can achieve to a wider audience. Academic studies are often assumed to take precedence over social needs, and this insensitivity results in loss of information that would be of interest to people beyond the academy, if time were taken and an effort made to engage with their concerns and sensitivities (Smith 2015).

Trophy heads: During the 19th century there was an increased awareness of the 'scientific' place of the Bushmen as curiosities. So different were they perceived to be that museums and their curators vied to obtain examples of Khoisan

199

people for their collections. This resulted in grotesque activities, such as the donation of heads by colonial officers in response to requests from European institutions.

This frenzy for collecting 'Bushman' skulls and skeletons was a consequence of the idea that the Bushmen were a 'dying race', and that museums needed to act fast to obtain examples before they disappeared. There were outrageous statements made, such as the tongue-in-cheek editorial that appeared in Kimberley's *Diamond Fields Advertiser* on 18 February 1907:

> [T]he Bushmen are disappearing from the face of the land that once was theirs, and in a few years will be as extinct as the dodo. In consequence of a fate that is inevitable, we have it on the best authority that more than one European museum would only be too glad of a 'specimen' or two. If therefore, any reader should know of a docile Bushman who has no particular use for himself, the scientific world would be truly grateful if that same Bushman could be induced to pack himself in formalin, or something of the sort, and ship himself to Europe for the purposes of ornamenting a dust-proof case, side by side with the mummies of Egypt. And we can promise him this distinction, that many an honest white man will have to be satisfied with a much less honourable use for his mortal coil. (Legassick & Rassool 2000: 4)

On occasion of retaliation against stock theft or murder by Bushmen, the perpetrator was often shot, and his head cut off to be sent to Europe, where they became known as 'trophy heads'. Such heads are known to have existed (and many still exist) in institutions in Geneva (Eric Huysecom, personal communication), Vienna (Legassick & Rassool 2000), Germany, Oxford, Cambridge, London (Skotnes 1996) and Edinburgh (Morris 1996).

The idea of exhibiting the 'Bushmen' continued right up to the 1950s. In 1952, during the Van Riebeeck Festival, held to mark 300 years of white colonialism, a group of ten Bushmen were brought from then South West Africa (Namibia) and put on display in Cape Town. The idea of displaying 'natives' to contrast with the 'civilising' space given to the colonists was highly controversial among coloured people at the time (Rassool & Witz 2017).

Forced removals

There were several areas around Cape Town where working-class coloured people lived before apartheid. Most were close to the city centre, where people worked, such as the Bo-Kaap and District Six, as well as Harfield Village and Newlands on the other side of Table Mountain. All of this was disrupted by the Group Areas Act of 1950 (and subsequent amendments), which identified the best areas for 'white' people to live, to the exclusion of all others classified differently. The removal of people from District Six and their relocation much further out of town, on the Cape Flats, used the excuse that District Six was a slum area in need of renewal.

This social disruption cannot be fully understood unless one considers the increased cost to poorer people of getting to work, but more important was the loss of social space. While District Six may have been an economically poorer community, it was rich in social support. Families who had lived together for many generations were split apart, losing the immediate cohesion that offered mutual help, such as grannies taking care of their grandchildren to allow parents to go to work, or fixing things in the houses, such as electrical or paint work.

The shops in District Six were mostly locally owned and serviced. As an outsider, I did not fully understand the implications of this at the time until Mr Vassen, who skilfully repaired my climbing boots in his shop on Hanover Street, had to close because the building was to be demolished in 1977. He had to move to the Oriental Plaza, which, because of all the removals, was not in the centre of his client base any more.

The removals and demolition of District Six were not dissimilar to what was happening to inner-city families in Glasgow, London and other parts of the United Kingdom, where no sociologists or anthropologists were included with the city planners or architects to understand the social implications of the transition (see Young & Willmott 1962). At least in the UK the participants went willingly, and not by force, as was the case in apartheid South Africa.

Today, almost three decades into the democratic era, much of the area of District Six still stands empty, and the older generation are dying without seeing 'their' land coming back to them.

The colonial gaze

The study of the Khoisan has always been from the outside looking in. We can see this in the placement of the Bushmen among the stuffed wild animals of Africa in the South African Museum (while 'civilised' people, such as Ancient Egyptians, were in the nearby Cultural History Museum), in the sending of Bushman trophy heads to foreign museums (Legassick & Rassool 2000), in the classification of the Bushmen at the very bottom of the 'Great Chain of Being', the human evolutionary ladder (Lovejoy 1942), or in the killing of Bushmen as vermin (Adhikari 2010). Even the study of the Bushmen in the field was a bit like a study of wild African game animals. The more prominent of the anthropologists have been very sensitive to the needs of their Bushman informants, and, having spent many years in the field, could speak the language. But even they knew they could always leave and return to their First World homes and offices.

This inevitably leads us to the ethics of studying people who have very little idea what anthropologists do or how they might use the information they collect. This question is even more acute when thinking about geneticists who collect blood samples, take them back to the lab and write papers that are published in reputable, peer-reviewed journals, from which they get further research funds or promotion.

In an increasingly globalised world, only sensitive ethical behaviour can help to bridge the divide. But even sensitivity has problems filling the gaps being created by schools where learning potentially will allow Third World children a space to live (if not compete) as the outside world encroaches on the lives that their parents are often not equipped to deal with. Schools are not necessarily easy places to find one's space. I once worked with a bright young Bushman schoolboy in Namibia who said the other black children at his 'mixed' school looked down on him for being just a 'Bushman'.

The growth of tourism (and the rise of the 4x4 vehicle) is generally not very sensitive to the needs of isolated people who would like to maintain their traditional lifestyle. Or is this just a dream of wilderness, which really does not exist any more?

The Khoisan legacy

What this book has tried to do is to offer some information about what might have existed before the colonial intrusion. This is not just an academic exercise, because the values that held Khoisan societies together are important, even in the 21st century. The social conditions of hunters described here would have been what existed throughout the world before the advent of food production, some 12 000 years ago.

It might be argued that the picture we have of hunter-gatherers from 20th-century social anthropology is a modern vision, and it might have been somewhat different 2 000 years ago, when the first herders arrived in southern Africa. I would suggest, however, not only that it is the best we have but that the changes were probably minimal, at least from a social perspective of how people dealt with each other. There is no way that archaeology, even at its best, can offer such detail. For the Khoekhoen, things are even more difficult, because their society was ripped apart 300 years ago, and the observations from that time are limited and seen through the colonial prism. Archaeology offers a good base, and, along with linguistics and DNA analyses, is starting to fill many of the gaps in our understanding.

I have tried to show that the social norms of egalitarianism in Bushman society have relevance for our society today, where overconsumption is lauded. Think of a society with no leaders – everyone on the same level, your ego subsumed into the common good. This is the way the Bushmen would have expected people to act. Perhaps the biggest threat to such a society is our ubiquitous television advertising, where viewers are bombarded with images of foreign-made goods that most would like but probably do not need. Television and social media have influenced how ideas spread and are controlled by mass marketing, implying that if you don't have a Breitling watch, or drive a Mercedes-Benz, then you haven't 'made it'. This is made even worse by the global spread of the smartphone, which is now more easily available than the traditional land-line telephone, especially in the developing world where national telephone systems only ever had a limited distribution. Today there is little chance of getting lost, because GPS-based tracking systems are available everywhere. But remember: traditional hunter-gatherers and herders never get lost, because they are in tune with the land around them.

Among the Khoekhoen, although there existed the larger 'tribal' organisation, such as the Cochoqua or Namaqua, the real power was vested in a collective of family groups, or clans, which were exogamous, that is, marriage had to be outside the clan. These groups were organised hierarchically and the leader of the 'tribal' group was 'acknowledged to be head of the senior clan ... but the heads of other clans acted as his council, and he could not do much without their cooperation' (Schapera 1930: 227). 'The functions of the chief ... were purely political ... and he presided over the tribal council. The latter was the real governing body of the tribe' (Ibid: 328). Thus, '[t]he chief of the tribe was little more than *primus inter pares*' (first among equals) (Ibid: 227).

Among the Khoekhoen clans there was a degree of fluidity, and this would have affected leadership. If there was competition within the clan, one group could break off and follow a different leader, basically 'voting with their feet'. If this was indeed the case, then the social order among both the southern African hunters and herders was similar in that it required the ability to negotiate among group members to reach a communal decision, which depended on respect rather than simply a hereditary leadership position. Leadership may have been hereditary among the Khoe, but during the colonial period it was cemented by Dutch authorities, who gave staffs of office to individuals they wanted to be able to negotiate with, giving 'the "captain" a more prominent position as an individual than he really seems to have occupied in the original conditions of native life' (Ibid: 331).

An example of this would be the dispute over leadership between the Chainoqua and Hessequa clans in the Overberg during Simon van der Stel's governorship at the end of the 17th century. Koopman gained ascendency over Klaas or Dorha within the Chainoqua (Elphick 1985) and in time his name became used by that clan. The fight between the two clans continued under British occupation, as observed by Latrobe (1818), who was asked to mediate. The British authorities recognised the Koopman clan instead of the Hessequa in the area. This consolidated leadership on European feudal principles, and so became a colonial artefact.

Yes, these ideas of society are small-scale, but we are bombarded by religious and political egos, all convinced that we need to know their 'story' (as Harari 2018 would say). Can the aboriginal Khoisan help us get beyond this? Can Khoisan leaders get beyond this? Or do people need the ranting of so-called populists to lead the way? We have only to see the grotesque behaviour of Donald Trump during the COVID-19 pandemic disaster to see how a narcissistic leader can derail scientific knowledge and experience in favour of his own re-election campaign.

Perhaps all is not lost. If a young Swedish girl can stand up for global climate change needs, then is there a respected Khoisan leader who could offer a better way to raise issues such as poor education for their descendants in South Africa, and to demand a better quality of life, including housing, health and job security? It is only with an educated population that real aspirations towards a middle-class lifestyle can be achieved.

If we go back to the resilience-theory model discussed in Chapter 7, we can see that the r phase (growth) is the crucial one (see Table 7.1). This is where problem areas should be identified and ways to rectify them discussed. This is what the world-wide climate demonstrations are all about: there are massive 'cracks' in the system due to inequality and access to resources. If barriers are put up, the transition to the K phase (conservation) will not be inclusive, and the system (economic or social) could go into a dive, which starts the feedback loop all over again.

In South Africa, hereditary leadership along patriarchal tribal lines without democratic principles does nothing to benefit large numbers of rural people, particularly women, who are the ones who have to work the land and feed their families, and, again, deal with a dysfunctional education system. The extension of the National House of Traditional Leaders Act to include Khoe and San (passed by Parliament as the Traditional and Khoi-San Leadership Act 3 of 2019) represents an entrenchment of the African patriarchy, excluding women's right to land, and an extension of feudal institutions of colonial staffs of office and apartheid Bantustan policies. If these leaders are not elected, would they not be outside the realm of good democratic governance? This is an important exclusionary 'crack' that needs filling.

As I said at the beginning of this book, Khoekhoen played an important role in world history. It is time for Khoisan to be celebrated as a crucial part of southern Africa's past. To Khoisan descendants: this is your history, be proud of where you came from, and where it may take you.

> For all the so-called advances and advantages of modern civilisation we have to be aware that something important has been lost in the process. Many of us, perhaps too many, have lost our sense of wildness.
>
> *— Ian McCallum, 2005*

APPENDIX

Medicinal Plants Used by the Descendants of Khoekhoen in South Africa

The lists given below would have been pharmacopoeia used for many centuries. Some would even have been passed on by Sonqua healers to the Khoekhoen, if, as suggested in Chapter 7, the men who arrived with the first domestic animals took local women as wives.

Medicinal plants used in Namaqualand
(after Archer 1994; Van Wyk & Gericke 2018)

According to Archer (1994: 66), herbaceous plants 'are used for influenza, for pains and aches and for stomach ailments. Herbalists-healers travel extensively to get appropriate herbs and people who visit family or friends will often return home with some of the local herbs. Herbs are also sent to family and friends in other areas who need particular remedies, illustrating that plants which are used medicinally in any specific locality may have been harvested far away. Although certain popular plants do not occur in all of the areas it is common for people to know about some of the more popular species.'

209

She says that 20 plants are used regularly, but was unable to identify three of them: rabas, galbos and griepbos. If we look below we will see that rabas was identified in the Overberg as *Pelargonium grossularioides*.

Species	Part used	Uses
Vachellia erioloba	bark	
Vachellia karroo	bark from branches	
Vachellia karroo	bark from roots	haemorrhage, dysentery, diarrhoea
Aloe dichotoma	roots	
Aloe pearsonii	leaves	
Annesorrhiza altiscapa	roots	
Antizoma miersiana	roots	
Apiosimum sp	leaf stem	
Arctotis aspera	leaves	
Gomphocarpus fruticosus	latex, leaves	sedative, head-ache, emetic
Gomphocarpus fruticosus	fresh/dried roots	abdominal pains
Ballota africana	leaves	fever, flu, measles, asthma, head-ache, stress, kidney/bladder infection
Boscia albitrunca	leaves	epilepsy

Boscia albitrunca	roots	
Cotyledon orbiculata	stem	sore throat, worming, boils, abscesses, nappy rash, epilepsy, tooth/earache
Crassula elegans	roots	
Crassula muscosa	leaves	
Cyperus marginatus	roots	
Cyphia phyteum	roots	
Dicoma capensis	leaves	fever, colds, flu, hypertension, diarrhoea, cancer
Diospyros lyciodes	roots	antibiotic chewing stick
Euclea pseudebenus	roots	chewing stick
Galium tomentosum	roots	
Gorteria diffusa		
Hermannia stricta	leaves	
Hypertelis saisoloides	leaves	
Mentha longifolia	leaves	respiratory ailments, headaches, epilepsy, fever, indigestion, urinary tract
Nicotiana glauca	leaves	headaches, pain relief

Nymania capensis	leaves	
Oxalis pes-caprae	leaves	
Pelargonium antidysentericum	caudex	
Pteronia luciliodes	leaves	
Rhus burchellii	leaves	
Ricinus communis	leaves, seeds	purgative, wounds, toothache
Salix mucronata		rheumatism, fever
Salvia dentata	leaves	colds, flu, bronchitis, abdominal pain
Monsonia crassicaule	branches	fire lighting
Monsonia patersonii	stem	
Sarcostemma viminale	latex	milk flow in mothers
Lessertia frutescens	roots	fever, indigestion
Lessertia frutescens	leaves	kidney/liver complaints
Tamarix usneoides	roots	firewood
Tulbaghia dregeana	leaves	
Tulbaghia dregeana	corms	
Ziziphus mucronata	bark/leaves	diarrhoea, dysentery
Ziziphus mucronata	roots	chest problems

Medicinal plants used in the Overberg

Report in *Het Volksblad*, Tuesday, 29 December 1885 (translated from Dutch/Afrikaans):

'The Reverend Mr Hettasch, Genadendal, compiled the following list of herbs used by indigenous people for medicinal purposes and of which samples shall be sent to the Colonial Exhibition 1886 in London. The botanical names have been added by Prof MacOwen.'

1a. Kleine Bels (*Osmitopsis dentata*, Cass).
Grows in the mountains.

1b. Groote Bels (*Osmitopsis asteriscoides*, Cass)
Grows along watercourses. Both Kleine and Groote Bels are boiled in water or put in brandy. From infusions, take three times a day several drops or up to half a small cup to create perspiration against colds, coughs and worms. Kleine Bels is stronger than Groote Bels.

2. Bok – Buchu (*Agathosma virgata*, BW), Bokboegoe (*Diosoma hirsuta*)
Grows along the top of mountains. From infusions three times a day one small cup. Against fever, chest pain and cough.

3. Wilde Salie (*Salvia aurea* L)
Grows in kloofs along water. From infusions three times a day one small cup. Against menstruation, cough and to make you perspire.

4. Ysterbosch (*Dodonea viscosa* EZ)
Grows on mountains. From infusions three times a day one small cup. Against high blood pressure, tuberculosis and chest pain.

5. Rabas (*Pelargonium grossularioides*, Ait var)
   Grows in valleys. From infusions three times a day one
   small cup. Against missed menstruation. Mixed with
   no 7, Wilde sellerij, not too strong, for improvement of
   bleeding after giving birth.

6. Kruizement (*Mentha longifolia* L)
   Grows in valleys along water. From infusions three times
   a day one small cup, as hot as possible. Against colds,
   missed menstruation, improvement of bleeding after
   given birth. For children against coughs, grind the herb
   fine, mix with honey and put on to tongue.

7. Wilde sellerij, fine and coarse (*Notabubon galbanum L*) =
   Blister Bush
   From infusions three times a day one small cup, but not
   strong. Against colds, bleeding, and for perspiration.

8. Berg Buchu (*Agosthosme crenulata*, Hook)
   Grows on mountains. From infusions three times a day
   one small cup. Against chest pains, fever in children,
   ground like flour give one measure with honey.

9. Hottentots kooigoed (*Helichrysum crispum*, Less)
   Grows in valleys. Add to bath water against colds.
   Mixed with no 3, 5, 6, 7 for mothers after childbirth.

10. Xaiboschjes (*Helichrysum serpyllifolium*, Less)
    Grows along rivers. Infusions not too strong. Against
    vaginal discharge, against faintness by covering your
    head and perspire over a bowl.

11. Turksche nagelties (*Pelargonium grossularioides*, Ait var)
    (see also no 5)
    Grows along rivers. Infusions. Against confusion and a
    tight chest.

12. Misbredie (*Chenopodium murale*, L) (marog)
    Grows along rivers. Infusions, also pound the green
    leaves and give the juice to children in drops; against
    fever, stomach ache and flatulence.

13. Hondepisbossie (*Exomis microphylla* Fenzl)
    Grows on old land. Infusions or green leaves pounded.
    Against inflammations: mixed with no 12.

14. Hederich (*Stachys aethiopicus*, L) (kleinkatterkruise
    Grows along rivers. With sugar boiled to syrup. Three
    times a day one teaspoon. Against whooping cough and
    other coughs.

15. Bitterboschje (*Chironia baccifera*, L)
    Grows on hills. Infusion three times a day one small cup,
    not too strong. Against cough, tuberculosis and missed
    menstruation.

16. Geneesboschje (*Hermannia cuneifolia* var *cuneifolia*) (see
    Bulbine frutescens)
    Grows on old ground, stamped by cattle. Pounded and
    applied to fresh wounds and left there until it falls off.

17. Paarden voetje (*Centella asiatica*)
    Grows along water. Pounded and the juice is used with
    alum against sore mouth.

18. Kissiblaar (*Malva parvifolia, Lf*) not ZA origin?
    Grows in gardens. Infusion is put in bath water against
    high fever in children. After the bath take one teaspoon.

19. Miergras (*Anagallis arvensis* subsp *coerulea*) not ZA origin?
    Grows in gardens. Boiled until thickened like porridge
    and put on to wounds to open them.

20. Stinkkruiden (*Chenopodium ambrosioides L*) (see *Oncosiphon
    suffruticosum*)

Grows in gardens. Green leaves are used against swellings.

21. Kaneelbol (*Pelargonium triste* L) (Kaneeltjies)
     Grows in hills. The corm is boiled, three times a day,
     one small cup is used against high blood pressure.

22. Watergras (*Persicaria decipiens*)
     Grows along water. Infusion. Taken three times a day,
     one small cup against vaginal discharge.

23. Klaasloo Bakbos (*Nidorella ivifolia*)(see *Conuza scabrida*)
     Grows in gardens. The flowers are boiled with sugar
     until syrup. One teaspoon on empty stomach in the
     morning against worms.

24. Wij ruit (*Ruta graveolens*) not ZA origin?
     Grows in gardens. Infusion. Drops against wounds and
     constipation, small cups against high blood pressure in
     adults.

25. Wilde als (*Artemisia afra* Jacq)
     Grows in kloofs. Infusion against headache, cough,
     toothache and fainting.

26. Kruidje roer mij niet (*Melianthus major* L)
     Grows in valleys. Infusions are used against worms, for
     internal and external use, also in bathwater.

27. Klip dagga (*Leonotis ocymifolia*) (E Mey)
     Grows on hills. Infusion, three times a day, half a small
     cup against coughs and lung ailments.

28. Kalmus (*Cyperus* sp) (see *Acorus calamus*)
     Grows in water. Used like no 27. Against stomach ache
     and fever in bathwater.

29. Zoethout (*Rafnia amplexicaulis* Thbg)
     Grows on certain lands. Used like no 27 against stomach
     cramps.

30. Vogelent (*Viscum capense* L)

    Grows on *Rhus* species. Infusion, 12 to 15 drops against convulsions in children and fever.

31. Guarison (*Euclea undulata*) (guarri)

    Grows on mountains. Infusion, three times a day one small cup against chest pain and missed menstruation.

32. Lidjesgras (*Persicaria decipiens*)

    Grows along water. Used as no 31 against vaginal discharge.

33. Fijne als (*Artemisia* sp)

    Infusion combined with no 14 against difficult urination and bleeding.

ACKNOWLEDGEMENTS

Over the past 50 years I have worked closely with African herdsmen and hunters who have given of their experience and knowledge. Sitting drinking tea in a Tuareg camp where I was made welcome by Souleymane ag Kiyou and his family after several hours in a camel saddle will always be a fine memory of working in Mali.

I would like to thank Mark Stoneking for the use of his genetic data from the Kalahari (Table 8.2), and Tom Gülde-mann for permission to use his very important historic outline of the development of Khoe language (Figure 8.1).

My thanks go to Duncan Bull, Rijksmuseum, Amsterdam, for kindly sending me the digitised Gordon Gallery, and to the Bell Heritage Trust, UCT, for allowing me to reproduce several of the Charles Davidson Bell drawings. Appreciation must also go to Keith and Colleen Begg for their permission to use the photograph of the lion sleeping under the rock art overhang in Niassa National Park, Mozambique.

I am indebted to the students and colleagues from the Department of Archaeology, University of Cape Town: John

Parkington, Nick van der Merwe, Simon Hall, Judy Sealy, Lita Webley, Belinda Mutti and many more, who, from the very beginning of my 30 years until retirement, were welcoming and a steady source of inspiration. My very first view of UCT and Devil's Peak was from the back of John Parkington's old Land Rover in 1977.

Andrew B Smith
Department of Archaeology, University of Cape Town
andrew.smith@uct.ac.za

REFERENCES

Abrahams, G. 1993. The Grand Parade, Cape Town: Archaeological excavations of the seventeenth-century Fort Goede Hoop. *South African Archaeological Bulletin* 48: 3–15.

Adhikari, M. 2010. *The Anatomy of a South African Genocide: The Extermination of the Cape San Peoples*. Cape Town: UCT Press.

Albrecht, M. et al. 2001. Oruwanje 95/1: A late Holocene stratigraphy in northwestern Namibia. *Cimbebasia* 17: 1–22.

Alexander, J. 1984. Early frontiers in southern Africa. In Hall, M. et al. (eds), *Frontiers: Southern African Archaeology Today*. Oxford: BAR International Series 207, pp. 12–23.

Alexander, J.E. 1838. *An Expedition of Discovery into the Interior of Africa*, 2 vols. London: Henry Colburn.

Ambrose, S.H. 1984. The introduction of pastoral adaptations to the highlands of East Africa. In Clark, J.D. & Brandt, S.A. (eds), *From Hunters to Farmers: The Causes and Consequences of Food Production in Africa*. Berkeley: University of California Press, pp. 212–239.

Aparta, C. & Higgs, E.S. 2005. Global positioning systems, Inuit wayfinding, and the need for a new account of technology. *Current Anthropology* 46 (5).

Archer, F.M. 1994. Ethnobotany of Namaqualand: The Richtersveld. Unpublished MA thesis, University of Cape Town.

221

Arthur, C. 2008. The archaeology of indigenous herders in the Western Cape of southern Africa. *Southern African Humanities* 20 (1): 205–220.

Ashley, C.Z. & Grillo, K.M. 2015. Archaeological ceramics from eastern Africa: Past approaches and future directions. *Azania* 50 (4): 460–480.

Axelson, E. 1973. *Portuguese in South-East Africa 1488–1600*. Cape Town: Struik.

Badenhorst, S. 2018. Exploitation of sheep (*Ovis aries*) and goats (*Capra hircus*) by Iron Age farmers in southern Africa. *Quaternary International* 495: 79–86.

Balasse, M. et al. 2002. The seasonality mobility model for prehistoric herders in the south-western Cape of South Africa assessed by isotopic analysis of sheep enamel. *Journal of Archaeological Science* 29: 917–932.

Balasse, M. et al. 2003. Determining birth seasonality by analysis of tooth enamel oxygen isotope ratios: The Late Stone Age site of Kasteelberg (South Africa). *Journal of Archaeological Science* 30: 205–215.

Barbieri, C. et al. 2014. Unraveling the complex maternal history of southern African Khoisan populations. *American Journal of Physical Anthropology* 153: 435–448.

Barnard, A. 1992. *Hunters and Herders of Southern Africa: A Comparative Ethnography of the Khoisan Peoples*. Cambridge: Cambridge University Press.

——. 2002. The foraging mode of thought. In: Stewart, H., Barnard, A. & Omura, K. (eds), *Self and Other Images of Hunter-Gatherers*. Osaka: National Museum of Ethnology, pp. 5–24.

——. 2007. From Mesolithic to Neolithic modes of thought. In Whittle, A. & Cummings, V. (eds), *Going Over: The Mesolithic-Neolithic Transition in North-West Europe*. Proceedings of the British Academy 144: 5–19.

Barrow, J. 1801, 1804. *An Account of Travels into the Interior of Southern Africa in the Years 1797 and 1798*, 2 vols. London: Cadell & Davies.

Beaumont, P.B., Smith, A.B. & Vogel, J.C. 1995. Before the Einiqua: The archaeology of the frontier zone. In Smith, A.B. (ed.), *Einiqualand: Studies of the Orange River Frontier*. Cape Town: UCT Press, pp. 236–264.

Begg, C.M. et al. 2005. Ecological observations from a portion of the Lugenda Valley, Niassa Reserve: Resource utilization and densities of key animal species. Sociedade para a Gestão e Desenvolvimento da Reserva do Niassa, Moçambique.

Bleek, W.H.I. & Lloyd, L. 1911. *Specimens of Bushman Folklore*. London: Allen.

Blundell, G. 2004. *Nqabayo's Nomansland: San Rock Art and the Somatic Past*. Uppsala: Studies in Global Archaeology 2.

Boonzaier, E. et al. 1996. *The Cape Herders: A History of the Khoikhoi of Southern Africa*. Cape Town: David Philip.

Boucher, M. & Penn, N. 1992. *Britain at the Cape, 1795–1803*. Johannesburg: The Brenthurst Press.

Brelsford, W.V. 1946. *Fishermen of the Bangweulu Swamps: A Study of the Fishing Activities of the Unga Tribe*. The Rhodes-Livingstone Papers, 12.

Breton, G. et al. 2014. Lactase persistence alleles reveal partial East African ancestry of southern African Khoe pastoralists. *Current Biology* 24: 852–858. doi: 10.1016/j.cub.2014.02.041.

Brink, Y. 2004. The transformation of indigenous societies in the south western Cape during the rule of the Dutch East India Company, 1652–1795. In Murray, T. (ed.), *The Archaeology of Contact in Settler Societies*. Cambridge: Cambridge University Press, pp. 91–108.

Broadhurst, C.L. et al. 2002. Brain-specific lipids from marine, lacustrine, or terrestrial food resources: Potential impact on early

African *Homo sapiens. Comparative Biochemistry and Physiology Part B: Biochemistry and Molecular Biolo*gy 131 (4): 653–673.

Brook, G.A. et al. 2010. A 35 ka pollen and isotope record of environmental change along the southern margin of the Kalahari from stalagmite and animal dung deposits at Wonderwerk Cave, South Africa. *Journal of Arid Environments* 74: 870–884.

Bruner, E., Pereira-Pedro, A. & Bastir, M. 2017. Patterns of morphological integration between parietal and temporal areas of the human skull. *Journal of Morphology* 278 (10): 1312–1320. doi: 10.1002/jmor.20714.

Cashdan, E. 1986. Hunter-gatherers of the northern Kalahari. In Vossen, R. & Keuthmann, K. (eds), *Contemporary Studies on Khoisan I.* Hamburg: Helmut Buske Verlag, pp. 145–180.

Chan, E.K.F. et al. 2019. Human origins in a southern African palaeo-wetland and first migrations. *Nature* 575: 185–189. doi: 10.1038/s41586-019-1714-1.

Chevalier, M. & Chase, B.M. 2015. Southeast African records reveal a coherent shift from high-to-low-latitude forcing mechanisms along the east African margin across last glacial-interglacial transition. *Quaternary Science Reviews* 125: 117–130.

Chritz, K.L. et al. 2015. Environments and trypanosomiasis risks for early herders in the later Holocene of Lake Victoria Basin, Kenya. *Proceedings of the National Academy of Sciences* 112 (12): 3674–3679.

Coelho, M. et al. 2009. On the edge of Bantu expansions: mtDNA, Y chromosome and lactase persistence genetic variation in southwestern Angola. *BMC Evolutionary Biology* 9 (80). doi:10.1186/1471-2148/9/80.

Copley, M.S. et al. 2004. Organic residue evidence for the processing of marine animal products in pottery vessels from the pre-colonial archaeological site of Kasteelberg D east, South Africa. *South African Journal of Science* 100: 279–283.

Crader, D.C. 2008. Technology and classification of the grinding equipment. In Clark, J.D. et al., *Adrar Bous: Archaeology of a Central Saharan Granitic Ring Complex in Niger*. Tervuren: Royal Museum for Central Africa, Studies in Human Sciences 170: 291–311.

Cullinan, P. 1992. *Robert Jacob Gordon, 1743–1795: The Man and his Travels at the Cape*. Cape Town: Struik Winchester.

Da Costa, M.A.S. 1967. *Métodos e Apetrechos de Pesca*. Lourenço Marques: Gazeta do Agricultor, Publicações Série B: Divulgação 32.

Dahl, G. & Hjort, A. 1976. *Having Herds: Pastoral Herd Growth and Household Economy*. University of Stockholm, Department of Anthropology.

Dale, D. & Ashley, C.Z. 2010. Holocene hunter-fisher-gatherer communities: New perspectives on Kansyore using communities of Western Kenya. *Azania* 45 (1): 24–48.

Davison, P. 2018. The politics and poetics of the Bushman diorama at the South African Museum. ICOFOM Study Series 46: 81–97.

Deacon, J. 1986. 'My place is the Bitterpits': The home territory of Bleek and Lloyd's /Xam informants. *African Studies* 45 (2): 135–156.

De Jongh, M. 2012. *Roots and Routes: Karretjie People of the Great Karoo*. Pretoria: UNISA Press.

Denbow, J.R. 1990. Congo to Kalahari: Data and hypotheses about the political economy of the western stream of the Early Iron Age. *African Archaeological Review* 8: 139–175.

De Prada-Samper, J.M. 2016. *The Man Who Cursed the Wind*. Cape Town: African Sun Press.

Di Lernia, S. 1999. Discussing pastoralism: The case of the Acacus and surroundings (Libyan Sahara). *Sahara* 11: 7–20.

Dornan, S.S. 1925. *Pygmies and Bushmen of the Kalahari*. London: Seeley, Service.

Dowson, T.A. et al. 1994. A Stow site revisited: Zastron District, Orange Free State. In Dowson, T.A. & Lewis-Williams, D. (eds),

Contested Images: Diversity in Southern African Rock Art Research.
Johannesburg: Wits University Press, pp. 177–188.

Drury, J. & Drennan, M.R. 1926. The pudendal parts of the South
African Bush race. *Medical Journal of South Africa* 22: 113–117.

Dubow, S. 1995. *Illicit Union: Scientific Racism in Modern South Africa.*
Cambridge: Cambridge University Press.

Dunn, E.J. 1873. Through Bushmanland. *Cape Monthly Magazine*
(New Series) 6 (31): 31–42.

Dyson-Hudson, N. 1966. *Karimojong Politics.* Oxford: Oxford
University Press.

Eastwood, E. & Fish, W.S. 1996. Sheep in the rock paintings of the
Soutpansberg and Limpopo Valley. *Southern African Field Archaeology* 5 (2): 59–69.

Ehret, C. 1982. The first spread of food production to southern
Africa. In Ehret, C. & Posnansky, M. (eds), *The Archaeological and
Linguistic Reconstruction of African History.* Berkeley: University of
California Press, pp. 158–181.

Elphick, R. 1985. *Khoikhoi and the Founding of White South Africa.*
Johannesburg: Ravan Press.

Evans-Pritchard, E.E. 1940. *The Nuer.* Oxford: Oxford University
Press.

——. 1956. *Nuer Religion.* Oxford: Oxford University Press.

Fauvelle-Aymar, F.-X. 1999. Des murs d'Augsbourg aux vitrines du
Cap: Cinq siècles d'histoire du regard sur le corps des Khoisan.
Cahiers d'Études africaines 39 (155–156): 539–561.

——. 2008. Against the 'Khoisan paradigm' in the interpretation
of Khoekhoe origins and history: Re-evaluation of Khoekhoe
pastoral traditions. *Southern African Humanities* 20 (91): 77–92.

Fauvelle-Aymar, F.-X. et al. 2006. The visibility and invisibility of
herders' kraals in southern Africa, with reference to a possible
Early Contact Period Khoekhoe kraal at KFS 5, Western Cape.
Journal of African Archaeology 4 (2): 253–271.

Fewlass, H. et al. 2020. Chemical evidence of dairying by hunter-gatherers in highland Lesotho in the first millennium AD. *Nature Human Behaviour* 4: 791–799. doi.org/10.1038/s41562-020-0859-0.

Finnegan, E., Hart, T. & Halkett, D. 2011. The 'informal' burial ground at Prestwich Street, Cape Town: Cultural and chrono-logical indicators for the historical Cape underclass. *South African Archaeological Bulletin* 66 (194): 136–148.

Gibbon, V.E. & Davies, B. 2020. Holocene Khoesan health: A biocultural analysis of cranial pathology and trauma. *International Journal of Osteoarchaeology* 30 (3): 287–296. doi:10.1002/oa.2854: 110.

Gifford-Gonzalez, D. 2000. Animal disease challenges to the emer-gence of pastoralism in sub-Saharan Africa. *African Archaeological Review* 17 (3): 95–139.

———. 2016. 'Animal disease challenges' fifteen years later: The hypothesis in light of new data. *Quaternary International* 436 (Part A): 283–293. doi: 10.1016/j.quaint.2015.10.054.

Gil-Romera, G. et al. 2006. Middle-to-late-Holocene moisture changes in the desert of northwest Namibia derived from fossil hyrax dung pollen. *The Holocene* 16 (8): 1073–1084.

Goodwin, A.J.H. & Van Riet Lowe, C. 1929. The Stone Age Cultures of South Africa. *Annals of the South African Museum* 27: 1–289.

Grevenbroek, J.G. 1933. An Elegant and Accurate Account of the African Race living around the Cape of Good Hope commonly called Hottentots. In Schapera, I. & Farrington, E. (eds), *The Early Cape Hottentots, Described in the Writings of Olfert Dapper (1668), Willem ten Rhyne (1686) and Johannes Gulielmus de Grevenbroek (1695)*. Cape Town: Van Riebeeck Society no. 14: 161–299.

Grillo, K.M. et al. 2018. Pastoral Neolithic settlement at Luxmanda, Tanzania. *Journal of Field Archaeology* 43 (2): 102–120.

Grillo, K.M. et al. 2020. Molecular and isotopic evidence for milk, meat, and plants in prehistoric eastern African herder food systems. *Proceedings of the National Academy of Sciences* 117 (18): 9793–9799. doi:10.1073/pnas.1920309117//DCSupplemental.

Gronenborn, D. 2004. Comparing contact-period archaeologies: The expansion of farming and pastoralist societies to continental temperate Europe and to southern Africa. *Before Farming* 2004: 22–60.

Guenther, M. 1994. The relationship of Bushman art to ritual and folklore. In Dowson, T.A. & Lewis-Williams, D. (eds), *Contested Images: Diversity in Southern African Rock Art Research.* Johannesburg: Wits University Press, pp. 257–273.

Gugelberger, G.M. 1984. *Nama/Namibia: Diary and Letters of Nama Chief Hendrik Witbooi, 1884–1894.* Boston University African Studies Center, African Historical Documents Series no. 5.

Güldemann, T. 2006. Structural isoglosses between Khoekhoe and Tuu: The Cape as a linguistic area. In Matras, Y., McMahon, A. & Vincent, N. (eds), *Linguistic Areas: Convergence in Historical and Typological Perspective.* Basingstoke: Palgrave Macmillan, pp. 99–134.

——. 2008. A linguist's view: Khoe-Kwadi speakers as the earliest food-producers of southern Africa. *Southern African Humanities* 20 (1): 93–132.

Gulliver, P.H. 1951. *A Preliminary Survey of the Turkana.* School of African Studies, University of Cape Town, *Communications* New Series no. 26.

Gunderson, V.M. & Holling, C.S (eds). 2002. *Panarchy: Understanding Transformations in Human and Natural Systems.* New York: Island Press.

Haacke, W. 1982. Traditional hut-building technique of the Nama. *Cimbebasia* 3 (2): 77–98.

Hahn, T. 1881. *Tsuni-//Goam, The Supreme Being of the Khoi-Khoi.* London: Trübner.

Hall, M. 1986. The role of cattle in southern African agropastoral societies: More than bones can tell. In Hall, M. & Smith, A.B. (eds), *Prehistoric Pastoralism in Southern Africa*. South African Archaeological Society, Goodwin Series 5: 83–87.

Hall, S. 1986. Pastoral adaptations and forager reactions in the Eastern Cape. In Hall, M. & Smith, A.B. (eds), *Prehistoric Pastoralism in Southern Africa*. South African Archaeological Society, Goodwin Series 5: 42–49.

Hall, S. & Smith, B. 2000. Empowering places: Rock shelter and ritual control in farmer-forager interactions in the Northern Province. In Leslie, M. & Maggs, T. (eds), *African Naissance: The Limpopo Valley 1000 Years Ago*. South African Archaeological Society, Goodwin Series 8: 30–46.

Harari, Y.N. 2018. *21 Lessons for the 21st Century*. London: Jonathan Cape.

Henn, B.M. et al. 2008. Y-chromosomal evidence of a pastoralist migration through Tanzania to southern Africa. *Proceedings of the National Academy of Sciences* 105 (31): 10693–10698.

Henshilwood, C. 1996. A revised chronology for pastoralism in southernmost Africa: New evidence of sheep at c. 2000 BP from Blombos Cave, South Africa. *Antiquity* 70: 945–949.

Henshilwood, C. et al. 1994. Mussel drying and food storage in the late Holocene, south-west Cape. *Journal of Field Archaeology* 21: 103–109.

Henshilwood, C.S. et al. 2011. A 100,000-year-old ochre-processing workshop at Blombos Cave, South Africa. *Science* 334 (6053): 219–222. doi: 10.1126/science.1211535.

Hine, P. et al. 2010. Antiquity of stone-walled tidal fish traps on the Cape coast, South Africa. *South African Archaeological Bulletin* 65 (191): 35–44.

Hodder, I. 1981. *Symbols in Action*. Cambridge: Cambridge University Press.

Hoernlé, W.A. 1925. The social organisation of the Namaqua Hottentots of Southwest Africa. *American Anthropologist*, New Series 27 (1): 1–24.

Horsburgh, K.A. & Gosling, A. 2020. Systemic ancient DNA species identification fails to find Late Holocene domesticated cattle in Southern Africa. *Biology* 9 (10). doi: 10.3390/biology9100316.

Hublin, J. et al. 2017. New fossils from Jebel Irhoud, Morocco and the pan-African origin of *Homo Sapiens*. *Nature* 540: 289–292.

Hudson, N. 2004. 'Hottentots' and the evolution of European racism. *Journal of European Studies* 34 (4): 308–332.

Huffman, T.N. 2021. *Bambata* pottery and Western Bantu: Re-interpreting the Early Iron Age in southern Africa. *Southern African Humanities* 34: 1–17.

Hutton, C.W. 1887. *The Autobiography of the Late Sir Andries Stockenstrom, Bart*, 2 vols. Cape Town: Juta.

Ingold, T. 2000. *The Perception of the Environment: Essays on Livelihood, Dwelling and Skill*. London: Routledge.

Jacobsohn, M. 1990. *Himba: Nomads of Namibia*. Cape Town: Struik.

Jerardino, A. & Yates, R. 1996. Preliminary results from excavations at Steenbokfontein Cave: Implications for past and future research. *South African Archaeological Bulletin* 51: 7–16.

Jerardino, A. et al. 2013. Settlement and subsistence patterns since the terminal Pleistocene in the Elands Bay and Lamberts Bay areas. In Jerardino, A., Malan, A. and Braun, D. (eds), *The Archaeology of the West Coast of South Africa*. Oxford: BAR International Series 2526, pp. 85–108.

Johnson, P., Bannister, A. & Wannenburgh, A. 1979. *The Bushmen*. Cape Town: Struik.

Katz, R. 1982. *Boiling Energy: Community Healing among Kalahari Kung*. Cambridge, Mass.: Harvard University Press.

Kinahan, J. 2016. Archaeological evidence of domestic sheep in the

Namib Desert during the first millennium AD. *Journal of African Archaeology* 14 (1): 7–17. doi: 10.3213/2191-5784-10280.

Klein, R.G. 1983. The stone age prehistory of southern Africa. *Annual Review of Anthropology* 12: 25–48.

——. 1989. *The Human Career: Human Biological and Cultural Origins.* Chicago: University of Chicago Press.

Klein, R.G. & Cruz-Uribe, K. 1989. Faunal evidence for prehistoric herder-forager activities at Kasteelberg, Western Cape province, South Africa. *South African Archaeological Bulletin* 44: 82–97.

Klein, R.G. & Steele, T.E. 2013. Archaeological shellfish size and late human evolution in Africa. *Proceedings of the National Academy of Sciences* 110 (27): 10910–10915. doi.org/10.1073/pnas.1304750110.

Kolb, P. 1731. *The Present State of the Cape of Good Hope*, 2 vols. London: Innys.

Lajoux, J.-D. 1963. *The Rock Paintings of Tassili.* London: Thames & Hudson.

Latrobe, C.I. 1818. *Journal of a Visit to South Africa in 1815, and 1816.* London: L.B. Seeley.

Leakey, L.S.B. 1936. *Stone Age Africa: An Outline of Prehistory in Africa.* London: H. Milford.

Lee, R.B. 1969. Eating Christmas in the Kalahari. *Natural History* (December): 14–22, 60–63.

——. 1979. *The !Kung San: Men, Women and Work in a Foraging Society.* Cambridge: Cambridge University Press.

Legassick, M. & Rassool, C. 2000. *Skeletons in the Cupboard: South African Museums and the Trade in Human Remains 1907–1917.* Cape Town: South African Museum.

Leitch, S. 2009. Burgkmair's peoples of Africa and India (1508) and the origins of ethnography in print. *The Art Bulletin* 91 (2): 134–159.

Le Quellec, J.L. 2011. Provoking lactation by the insufflation technique as documented by the rock images of the Sahara. *Anthropozoologica* 46 (1): 65–125.

Le Roux, W. & White, A. 2004. *Voices of the San.* Cape Town: Kwela Books.

Lewin-Robinson, A.M. 1973. *The Letters of Lady Anne Barnard Written to Henry Dundas from the Cape of Good Hope, 1793–1803.* Cape Town: Balkema.

Lewis-Williams, J.D. 1981. *Believing and Seeing: Symbolic Meanings in Southern San Rock Paintings.* Cambridge: Cambridge University Press.

Lewis-Williams, J.D. & Dowson, T. 1989. *Images of Power: Understanding Bushman Rock Art.* Johannesburg: Southern Book Publishers.

Leyland, J. 1866. *Adventures in the Far Interior of South Africa, including a Journey to Lake Ngami.* London: George Routledge & Sons.

Liebenberg, L. 1990. *The Art of Tracking: The Origin of Science.* Cape Town: David Philip.

Lombard, M. 2020a. The tip cross-sectional areas of poisoned bone arrowheads from southern Africa. *Journal of Archaeological Science: Reports* 33 (102477). doi.org/10.1016/j.jasrep.2020.102477.

——. 2020b. Testing for poisoned arrows in the Middle Stone Age: A tip cross-sectional analysis of backed microliths from Southern Africa. *Journal of Archaeological Science: Reports* 34, Part A (102630). doi.org/10.1016/j.jasrep.2020.102630.

Lovejoy, A.O. 1942. *The Great Chain of Being.* Cambridge, Mass.: Harvard University Press.

Low, C. 2014. Khoe-San ethnography, 'new animism' and the interpretation of southern African rock art. *South African Archaeological Bulletin* 69 (200): 164–172.

Macholdt, E. et al. 2014. Tracing pastoralist migrations to Southern Africa with lactase persistence alleles. *Current Biology* 24: 875–879. doi.1016/j.cub.2014.03.127.

Maclaren, P.I.R. 1958. *The Fishing Devices of Central and Southern Africa.* The Occasional Papers of the Rhodes-Livingstone Museum, 12.

Maingard, L.F. 1934. Linguistic approach to South African pre-history and ethnology. *South African Journal of Science* 31: 122–129.

Malan, A. et al. 2017. *Grave Encounters: Archaeology of the Burial Grounds, Green Point, South Africa.* Cape Town: ACO Associates.

Manhire, A. 1993. A report on the excavations at Faraoskop Rock Shelter in the Graafwater district of the south-western Cape. *South African Field Archaeology* 2 (1): 3–23.

Manning, K. et al. 2011. 4500-year-old domesticated pearl millet (*Pennisetum glaucum*) from the Tilemsi Valley, Mali: New insights into an alternative cereal domestication pathway. *Journal of Archaeological Science* 38 (2): 312–322.

Marshall, F. 2000. The origins and spread of domestic animals in East Africa. In Blench, R.M. & MacDonald, K.C. (eds), *The Origins and Development of African Livestock: Archaeology, Genetics, Linguistics and Ethnography*, pp. 191–221. London: UCL Press.

Marshall, J. & Ritchie, C. 1984. *Where Are the Ju/wasi of Nyae Nyae?: Changes in a Bushman society: 1958–1981.* Centre for African Studies, University of Cape Town, *Communications* no. 9.

Marshall, L. 1976. *The !Kung of Nyae Nyae.* Cambridge, Mass.: Harvard University Press.

Mazel, A.D. 1992. Early pottery from the eastern part of southern Africa. *South African Archaeological Bulletin* 47 (155): 3–7.

McCallum, I. 2005. *Ecological Intelligence: Rediscovering Ourselves in Nature.* Cape Town: Africa Geographic.

Mitchell, P. 1996. Sehonghong: The Late Holocene assemblages with pottery. *South African Archaeological Bulletin* 51: 17–25.

———. 2002. *The Archaeology of Southern Africa.* Cambridge: Cambridge University Press.

———. 2014. The canine connection II: Dogs and southern African herders. *Southern African Humanities* 26: 1–10.

233

Moodie, D. 1838–1842. *The Record, or, A Series of Official Papers Relating to the Condition and Treatment of the Native Tribes of South Africa*. Cape Town: Robertson.

Morris, A.G. 1996. Trophy skulls, museums and the San. In Skotnes, P. (ed.), *Miscast: Negotiating the Presence of the Bushmen*. Cape Town: UCT Press, pp. 67–79.

——. 2014. Going full circle on Khoekhoe origins. *The Digging Stick* 31 (1): 1–4.

Morris, A.G. et al. 2014. First ancient mitochondrial human genome from a pre-pastoralist southern African. *Genome Biology & Evolution* 6 (10): 2647–2653. doi.org/10.1093/gbe/evu202.

Mugai, A.W.T. et al. 2004. Origin and migration of sheep in Africa. Paper presented at the Human Genome Conference, Cairo.

Mugai, A.W.T. & Hanotte, O. 2013. The origin of African sheep: Archaeological and genetic perspectives. *African Archaeological Review* 30 (1): 39–50. doi: 10.1007/s10437-013-9129-0.

Mutti, B. 2006. Domestic space on Kasteelberg herder sites. In Smith, A.B. (ed.), *Excavations at Kasteelberg, and the Origins of the Khoekhoen in the Western Cape, South Africa*. Oxford: BAR International Series 1537, pp. 79–94.

Mutundu, K.K. 2010. An ethnoarchaeological framework for identification and distinction of Late Holocene archaeological sites in East Kenya. *Azania* 45 (1): 6–23.

Myburgh, P.J. 2013. *The Bushman Winter Has Come*. Cape Town: Penguin Books.

Neumann, K. et al. 2012. First farmers in the Central African rain-forest: A view from southern Cameroon. *Quaternary International* 249: 53–62.

Newton-King, S. 1986. Khoisan resistance to colonial expansion, 1700–1828. In Cameron, T. & Spies, S.B. (eds), *An Illustrated History of South Africa*. Johannesburg: Jonathan Ball Publishers, pp. 107–109.

Nienaber, G.S & Raven-Hart, R. 1970. *Johan Daniel Buttner: Accounts of the Cape/Natal/East Indies, 1716–1721*. Cape Town: Balkema.

Noonan, L. 1989. *John of Empoli and His Relations with Afonso de Albuquerque*. Lisbon: Ministério da Educação, Instituto de Investigação Científica Tropical.

Oliveira, S. et al. 2017. The maternal genetic history of the Angolan Namib Desert: A key region for understanding the peopling of southern Africa. *American Journal of Physical Anthropology*. doi: 10.1002/ajpa.23378.

Oliveira, S. et al. 2018. The role of matrilineality in shaping pattern of Y-chromosome and mtDNA sequence variation in southwest Angola. *European Journal of Human Genetics* 27: 475–483.

Olivier, E. 2006. Archives Khoisan: l'histoire comme champs de la musique. *Afrique et Histoire* 6: 193–222.

Orpen, J.M. 1874. A glimpse into the mythology of the Maluti Bushmen. *Cape Monthly Magazine* (New Series) 9 (49): 1–13.

Oruru, B. et al. 2020. The first track of cultural astronomy in Uganda: Perspectives of the Baganda, Bagisu, Banyoro and Langi. *African Journal of History and Culture* 12 (2): 35–48.

Pager, H. 1972. *Ndedema*. Portland: International Scholarly Book Services.

Parkington, J., Dlamini, N. & Rusch, N. 2015. *First People: Ancestors of the San*. Cape Town: Krakadouw Trust.

Parkington, J. & Paterson, A. In press. 2021. Cloaks and torsos: Image recognition, ethnography and male initiation events in the rock art of Western Cape. *Azania*.

Parsons, I. & Lombard, M. 2016. The power of women in dairying communities of eastern and southern Africa. *Azania* 52 (1): 33–48. doi.org/10.1080/0067270X.2016.1249589.

Patrick, M., Smith, A.B. & De Koning, A.J. 1985. Gas-liquid chromatographic analysis of fatty acids in food residues from ceramics found in the southwestern Cape, South Africa. *Archaeometry* 27: 231–246.

Penn, N. 2005. *The Forgotten Frontier: Colonist and Khoisan on the Cape's Northern Frontier in the 18th Century.* Cape Town: Double Storey Books.

Petersen, D.C. et al. 2013. Complex patterns of genomic admixture within southern Africa. *PLOS Genetics* 9 (3): e1003309. doi:10.1371/journal.pgen.1003309.

Pfeiffer, S. 2016. An exploration of interpersonal violence among Holocene foragers of southern Africa. *International Journal of Paleopathology* 13: 27–38.

Phillipson, D.W. 1989. The first South African pastoralists and the Early Iron Age. *Nsi* 6: 127–134.

———. 1993. *African Archaeology*, 2nd edition. Cambridge: Cambridge University Press.

Pickrell, J.K. et al. 2012. The genetic prehistory of southern Africa. *Nature Communications* 3 (1143). doi.org/10.1038/ncomms2140.

Pleurdeau, D. et al. 2012. 'Of sheep and men': Earliest direct evidence of caprine domestication in southern Africa at Leopard Cave (Erongo, Namibia). *PLOS ONE* 7 (7): e40340. doi.org/10.1371/journal.pone.0040340.

Poland, M., Hammond-Tooke, D. & Voigt, L. 2000. *The Abundant Herds: A Celebration of the Nguni Cattle of the Zulu People.* Cape Town: Fernwood Press.

Prendergast, M.E. 2010. Kansyore fisher-foragers and transitions to food production in East Africa: The view from Wadh Lang'o, Nyanza province, Western Kenya. *Azania* 45 (1): 83–111.

Prendergast, M.E. et al. 2013. Pastoral Neolithic sites on the Southern Mbulu Plateau, Tanzania. *Azania* 48 (4): 498–520.

Prendergast, M.E. et al. 2019. Ancient DNA reveals a multistep spread of the first herders into sub-Saharan Africa. *Science* 365 (3448). doi:10.1126/science.aaw6275.

Quinton, J.C. & Lewin Robinson, A.M. (eds). 1973. *François Le Vaillant: Traveller in South Africa, and His Collection of 165 Water-colour Paintings, 1781–1784*, 2 vols. Cape Town: Library of Parliament.

Rakel, F. 1894. *Völkerkunde*. Leipzig: Bibliographisches Institut.

Raper, P.E. & Boucher, M. 1988. *Robert Jacob Gordon: Cape Travels, 1777 to 1786*, 2 vols. Johannesburg: The Brenthurst Press.

Rassool, C. & Witz, L. 2017. The 1952 Jan van Riebeeck Tercentenary Festival: Constructing and contesting public national history in South Africa. In Witz, L., Minckley, G. & Rassool, C. (eds), *Unsettled History: Making South African Public Pasts*. Ann Arbor: University of Michigan Press, pp. 52–76.

Raven-Hart, R. 1967. *Before Van Riebeeck*. Cape Town: Struik.

———. 1971. *Cape Good Hope: 1652–1702*, 2 vols. Cape Town: Balkema.

Redman, C.L. & Kinzig, A.P. 2003. Resilience of past landscapes: Resilience theory, society, and the *longue durée*. *Conservation Ecology* 7 (1): 14. https://www.ecologyandsociety.org/vol7/iss1/art14/.

Riley, E. 2007. The hunting ground's doings: /Xam narratives of hunting, animals and the veld. In Skotnes, P. (ed), *Claim to the Country: The Archive of Wilhelm Bleek and Lucy Lloyd*. Johannesburg: Jacana, pp. 290–311.

Ritchie, G. 1990. Dig the Herders/Display the Hottentots: The Production and Presentation of Knowledge about the Past. Unpublished MA thesis, University of Cape Town.

Robbins, L.H. et al. 2008. Recent archaeological and paleontological research at Toteng, Botswana: Early domesticated livestock in the Kalahari. *Journal of African Archaeology* 6 (1): 131–149.

Robertshaw, P.T. 1990. *Early Pastoralists of South-Western Kenya*. Nairobi: British Institute in Eastern Africa, Memoir 11.

Robertshaw, P.T. et al. 1983. Shell middens on the shores of Lake Victoria. *Azania* 18: 1–43.

Rosenberg, K. & Trevathan, W. 1996. Bipedalism and human birth:

The obstetrical dilemma revisited. *Evolutionary Anthropology* 4 (5): 161–168.

Rudner, I. & Rudner, J. 1957. A. Sparrman's ethnographic collection from South Africa. *Smärre Medelanden*. Stockholm: Ethnographical Museum of Sweden 25.

Rudner, J. 1968. Strandloper pottery from South and South West Africa. *Annals of the South African Museum* 49 (2): 441–663.

Sadr, K. 1998. The first herders at the Cape of Good Hope. *African Archaeological Review* 15 (2): 101–132.

——. 2002. Ancient pastoralists in the Sudan and in South Africa. In: Jennerstrasse 8 (eds), *Tides of the Desert: Contributions to the Archaeology and Environmental History of Africa in Honour of Rudolph Kuper*. Cologne: Heinrich-Barth-Institut, pp. 471–483.

——. 2003. The Neolithic of southern Africa. *Journal of African History* 44: 195–209.

——. 2004. Feasting on Kasteelberg? Early herders on the west coast of South Africa. *Before Farming* 3: 167–183.

——. 2005. From foraging to herding: The west coast of South Africa in the first millennium AD. *Human Evolution* 20 (4): 217–230.

——. 2007. Early first millennium pastoralists on Kasteelberg? The UB/UCT excavation at KBA. *South African Archaeological Bulletin* 62 (186): 154–161.

——. 2015. Livestock first reached southern Africa in two separate events. *PLOS ONE* 10 (8): e0134215. doi:10.1371/journal.pone.0134215.

——. 2018. Arrival of ceramics at Kasteelberg on the west coast of South Africa. *South African Archaeological Bulletin* 73 (207): 51–63.

Sadr, K. et al. 2017. New radiocarbon dates and the herder occupation of Kasteelberg B, South Africa. *Antiquity* 91 (359): 1299–1313.

Sadr, K. & Fauvelle-Aymar, F.-X. 2006. Ellipsoid grinding hollows on the west coast of South Africa. *Southern African Humanities* 18 (2): 29–50.

Sadr, K. & Sampson, C.G. 2006. Through thick and thin: Early pottery in southern Africa. *Journal of African Archaeology* 4 (2): 235–252.

Sadr, K. & Smith A.B. 1991. On ceramic variation in the southwestern Cape, South Africa. *South African Archaeological Bulletin* 46 (154): 107–115.

Sampson, C.G. 1988. *Stylistic Boundaries Among Mobile Hunter-Foragers.* Washington, DC: Smithsonian Institution Press.

Schama, S. 1995. *Landscape and Memory.* London: Fontana Press.

Schapera, I. 1930. *The Khoisan Peoples of South Africa: Bushmen and Hottentots.* London: Routledge & Kegan Paul.

Schlebusch, C.M. 2010. Genetic Variation in Khoisan-Speaking Populations from Southern Africa. PhD thesis, Faculty of Health Sciences, University of the Witwatersrand.

Schlebusch, C.M, Lombard, M. & Soodyall, H. 2013. MtDNA control region variation affirms diversity and deep sub-structure in populations from southern Africa. *BMC Evolutionary Biology* 13 (56). doi.org/10.1186/1471-2148-13-56.

Schlebusch, C.M. et al. 2020. Khoe-San genomes reveal unique variation and confirm the deepest population divergence in *Homo sapiens. Molecular Biology Evolution* 37 (10): 2944–2954. doi: 10.1093/molbev/msaa 140.

Schmidt, S. 2020. Animals and spirits of the road in Nama and Damara folklore and folk belief. *South African Archaeological Bulletin* 75 (213): 120–127.

Schoville, B.J. et al. 2017. The performance of heat-treated silcrete backed pieces in actualistic and controlled complex projectile experiment. *Journal of Archaeological Science: Reports* 14: 302–317.

Schrire, C. & Deacon, J. 1989. The indigenous artifacts from Oudepost 1, a colonial outpost of the VOC at Saldanha Bay, Cape. *South African Archaeological Bulletin* 44: 105–113.

Schultze, L. 1928. *Zur Kenntnis des Körpers der Hottentotten und Buschmänner*. Jena: G. Fischer.

Schuster, S.C. et al. 2010. Complete Khoisan and Bantu genomes from southern Africa. *Nature* 463: 943–947.

Schweitzer, F.R. 1979. Excavations at Die Kelders, Cape Province, South Africa: The Holocene deposits. *Annals of the South African Museum* 78: 101–232.

Sealy, J.C. 2010. Isotopic evidence for the antiquity of cattle-based pastoralism in southernmost Africa. *Journal of African Archaeology* 8 (1): 65–81.

Sealy, J.C. & Yates, R. 1994. The chronology of the introduction of pastoralism to the Cape, South Africa. *Antiquity* 68 (258): 58–67.

Seitsonen, O. 2012. Pastoral Neolithic studies in northern Tanzania: An interim report on XRF and stable isotope analyses in the Engaruku area (2012). *Nyame Akuma* 77: 11–23.

Shaw, P.A. et al. 2003. Holocene fluctuations of Lake Ngami, Middle Kalahari: Chronology and responses to climatic change. *Quaternary International* 111 (1): 23–35.

Shell, R.C.-H. 1994. *Children of Bondage: A Social History of the Slave Society at the Cape of Good Hope, 1652–1838*. Johannesburg: Wits University Press.

Shriner, D. et al. 2018. Genetic ancestry of Hadza and Sandawe peoples reveals ancient population structure in Africa. *Genome Biology and Evolution* 10 (3): 875–882.

Silberbauer, G.B. 1981. *Hunter and Habitat in the Central Kalahari Desert*. Cambridge: Cambridge University Press.

Skoglund, P. et al. 2017. Reconstructing prehistoric African population structure. *Cell* 171: 1–13. doi.org/10.1016/j.cell.2017.08.049.

Skotnes, P. (ed.). 1996. *Miscast: Negotiating the Presence of the Bushmen*. Cape Town: UCT Press.

———. 2007. *Claim to the Country: The Archive of Wilhelm Bleek and Lucy Lloyd.* Johannesburg: Jacana.

Smith, A.B. 1984. Adaptive strategies of prehistoric pastoralists in the south-western Cape. In Hall, M. et al. (eds), *Frontiers: Southern African Archaeology Today.* Oxford: BAR International Series 207, pp. 131–142.

———. 1989. Khoikhoi susceptibility to virgin soil epidemics in the 18th century. *South African Medical Journal* 75: 25–26.

———. 1993. Different facets of the crystal: Early images of the Khoikhoi at the Cape, South Africa. In Hall, M. & Markell, A. (eds), *Historical Archaeology in the Western Cape, South Africa.* South African Archaeological Society, Goodwin Series 7: 8–20.

———. 1995. Drawings of the Khoikhoi at the Cape of Good Hope: An update and response to Schrire. *South African Archaeological Bulletin* 50: 83–86.

———. 1998. Khoesaan orthography. *South African Archaeological Bulletin* 53: 37–38.

———. 2005. *African Herders: Emergence of Pastoral Traditions.* Walnut Creek: Altamira Press.

———. 2006. *Excavations at Kasteelberg and the Origins of the Khoekhoen in the Western Cape, South Africa.* Oxford: BAR International Series 1537.

———. 2008. The Tenerian. In Clark, J.D. et al., *Adrar Bous: Archaeology of a Central Saharan Granitic Ring Complex in Niger.* Tervuren: Royal Museum for Central Africa, Studies in Human Sciences, 170: 201–243.

———. 2014. *The Origins of Herding in Southern Africa: Debating the 'Neolithic' Model.* Saarbrücken: Lambert Academic Publishing.

———. 2015. Repatriation begins at home: Violence against South Africa's underclass, a colonial legacy that needs closure. In Mayor, A. et al. (eds), *African Memory in Danger – Memoire africaine en péril. Journal of African Archaeology* Monograph Series, vol. 11.

Frankfurt: Africa Magna Verlag, pp. 52–60.

——. 2016. More thoughts on Khoekhoe origins. *The Digging Stick* 33 (1): 15–16.

——. 2017. Why would southern African hunters be reluctant food producers? *Hunter-Gatherer Research* 2 (4): 415–435.

Smith, A.B. & Begg, K.S. 2017. Stories and myths about the pre-Iron Age inhabitants of south-central Africa. *The Digging Stick* 34 (1): 7–9.

Smith, A.B. & Bull, D. 2016. Col. R.J. Gordon's observations on some cultural practices among the Khoekhoen in the late 18th century. *The Digging Stick* 33 (3): 1–5.

Smith, A.B. & Jacobson, L. 1995. Excavations at Geduld and the appearance of early domestic stock in Namibia. *South African Archaeological Bulletin* 50: 3–14.

Smith, A.B. & Kinahan, J. 1984. The invisible whale. *World Archaeology* 16 (1): 89–97.

Smith, A.B. & Pasche, W.E. 1997. Balthasar Springer at the Cape (1506). *Quarterly Bulletin of the South African Library* 51: 93–98.

Smith, A.B. & Pheiffer, R.H. 1992. Col. Robert Jacob Gordon's notes on the Khoikhoi 1779–80. *Annals of the South African Cultural History Museum* 5 (1): 1–56.

——. 1993. *The Khoikhoi at the Cape of Good Hope: Seventeenth-century drawings in the South African Library*. Cape Town: South African Library.

Smith, A.B. & Ripp, M.R. 1978. An archaeological reconnaissance of the Doorn/Tanqua Karoo. *South African Archaeological Bulletin* 33 (128): 118–128.

Smith, A.B. & Webley, L. 2000. Women and men of the Khoekhoen of southern Africa. In Hodgson, D. (ed.), *Rethinking Pastoralism: Gender, Culture and the Myth of the Patriarchal Pastoralist*. London: James Currey, pp. 72–96.

Smith, A.B., Malherbe, C., Guenther M. & Berens, P. 2000. *The*

Bushmen of Southern Africa: A Foraging Society in Transition. Cape Town: David Philip.

Smith, A.B., Woodborne, S., Lamprechts, E.C. & Riley, F.R. 1992. Marine mammal storage: Analysis of buried seal meat at the Cape, South Africa. *Journal of Archaeological Science* 19: 171–180.

Smith, B.W. & Ouzman, S. 2004. Taking stock: Identifying Khoekhoen herder rock art in southern Africa. *Current Anthropology* 45 (4): 499–515.

Smith, S.E. 1980. The environmental adaptation of nomads in the West African Sahel: A key to understanding prehistoric pastoralists. In Williams, M.A.J. & Faure, H. (eds), *The Sahara and the Nile*. Rotterdam: Balkema, pp. 467–487.

Solomon, A. 1995. Rock Art Incorporated: An Archaeological and Interdisciplinary Study of Certain Human Figures in San Art. Unpublished doctoral thesis, University of Cape Town.

Spear, T. & Waller, R. (eds). 1993. *Being Maasai*. London: James Currey.

Stander, P.E., Ghau, //, Tsisaba, D., ≠Oma, //, !Ui, /. 1997. Tracking and the interpretation of spoor: a scientifically sound method in ecology. *Journal of Zoology* 242: 329–341.

Strauss, T. 1979. *War Along the Orange: The Korana and the Northern Frontier Wars of 1868–9 and 1878–9*. Centre for African Studies, University of Cape Town, *Communications* no. 1.

Stow, G.W. 1905. *The Native Races of South Africa*. London: Swan Sonnenschein.

Suttles, W. 1960. Affinal ties, subsistence and prestige among the Coast Salish. *American Anthropologist* 62: 296–305.

Suzman, J. 2017. *Affluence without Abundance: The Disappearing World of the Bushmen*. New York: Bloomsbury.

The Hunters. 1957. [Film]. John Marshall. (dir.) Cambridge, Mass.: Film Study Center, Harvard University.

243

Thom, H.B. 1952–1958. *Journal of Jan van Riebeeck*, 3 vols. Cape Town: Balkema.

Thomas, E.M. 1969. *The Harmless People*. Harmondsworth: Penguin Books.

Tishkoff, S.A. et al. 2007. History of click-speaking populations of Africa inferred from mtDNA and Y-chromosome genetic variation. *Molecular Biology Evolution* 24: 2180–2195.

Tobias, P.V. 1971. The biology of the southern African Negro. In Hammond-Tooke, W.D. (ed.), *The Bantu-speaking Peoples of Southern Africa*, 2nd edition. London: Routledge & Kegan Paul, pp. 3–45.

Trudgen, R. 2000. *Why Warriors Lie Down and Die*. Darwin: Aboriginal Resource and Development Services, Inc.

Uren, C. et al. 2016. Fine-scale human population structure in southern Africa reflects ecogeographic boundaries. *Genetics* 204 (1): 303–314. doi.org.10.1534/genetics.116.187369.

Van der Walt, J. & Lombard, M. 2018. Kite-like structures in the Nama Karoo of South Africa. *Antiquity* 92363, e3: 1–6.

Van Wyk, B.-E. & Gericke, N. 2018. *People's Plants: A Guide to Useful Plants of Southern Africa*, revised edition. Pretoria: Briza.

Vinnicombe, P. 1976. *People of the Eland: Rock Paintings of the Drakensberg Bushmen as a Reflection of their Life and Thought*. Pietermaritzburg: Natal University Press.

Wadley, L. 1976. Radiocarbon dates from Big Elephant Shelter, Erongo Mountains, South West Africa. *South African Archaeological Bulletin* 31: 146.

Walker, N.J. 1983. The significance of an early date for pottery and sheep in Zimbabwe. *South African Archaeological Bulletin* 38: 88–92.

Waterhouse, G. 1932. *Simon van der Stel's Journal of his Expedition to Namaqualand 1685–6*. Dublin: Hodges, Figgis.

Watson, S. 1991. *Return of the Moon: Versions from the /Xam*. Cape Town: Carrefour Press.

Webley, L.E. 2001. The re-excavation of Spoegrivier Cave on the west coast of South Africa. *Annals of the Eastern Cape Museums* 2: 19–49.

Westphal, E.O.J. 1963. The linguistic prehistory of southern Africa: Bush, Kwadi, Hottentot, and Bantu linguistic relationships. *Africa* 33: 237–265.

Wiessner, P. 1996. Levelling the hunter: Constraints on the status quest in foraging societies. In Wiessner, P. & Schiefenhövel, W. (eds), *Food and the Status Quest: An Interdisciplinary Perspective.* Oxford: Berghahn Books, pp. 171–191.

Wilson, M. 1969. The Hunters and Herders. In Wilson, M. & Thompson, L. (eds), *The Oxford History of South Africa, Vol 1: South Africa to 1870.* Oxford: Oxford University Press, pp. 40–74.

Wittenberg, H. 2012. The Boer and the Jackal: Satire and resistance in Khoi orature. *Southern African Journal of Folklore Studies* 22 (1): 10–13.

Witz, L., Minkley, G. & Rassool, C. 2017a. Sources and genealogies of the new museum: The living fossil, the photograph, and the speaking subject. In Witz, L., Minckley, G. & Rassool, C. (eds), *Unsettled History: Making South African Public Pasts.* Ann Arbor: University of Michigan Press, pp. 177–203.

Witz, L., Rassool, C. & Minkley, G. 2017b. The Castle, the gallery, the sanatorium, and the petrol station: Curating a South African nation in the museum. In Witz, L., Minckley, G. & Rassool, C. (eds), *Unsettled History: Making South African Public Pasts.* Ann Arbor: University of Michigan Press, pp. 99–123.

Woodburn, J. 1988. African hunter-gatherer social organisation: Is it best understood as a product of encapsulation? In Ingold, T., Riches, D. & Woodburn, J. (eds), *Hunters and Gatherers, Vol 1: History, Evolution and Social Change.* Oxford: Berg, pp. 31–64.

Wright, D. 2013. Fits and starts: why did domesticated animals 'trickle' before they 'splashed' into Sub-Saharan Africa? In Baldia, M.O., Perttula, T. & Frink, D. (eds), *Comparative*

Archaeology and Palaeoclimatology: Socio-cultural Responses to a Changing World. Oxford: BAR International Series 2456, pp. 63–81.

Yates, R., Parkington, J. & Manhire, T. 1990. *Pictures from the Past: A History of the Interpretation of Rock Paintings and Engravings of Southern Africa.* Pietermaritzburg: Centaur Publications.

Yellen, J. 1984. The integration of herding into prehistoric hunting and gathering economies. In Hall, M. et al. (eds), *Frontiers: Southern African Archaeology Today.* Oxford: BAR International Series 207, pp. 53–64.

Young, M. & Willmott, P. 1962. *Family and Kinship in East London.* Harmondsworth: Penguin.

INDEX